CONTENTS

ACKNOWLEDGEMENTS

We are indebted to the staff and pupils in the five case study schools who so willingly gave up their time to be interviewed.

Our thanks are also extended to members of the project's Steering Group, chaired by Professor Eric Bolton, who have made valuable contributions throughout this phase of the study.

We would also like to thank Mary Ashworth, Jay Day and Nick Whybrow, who undertook some of the fieldwork in the five case study schools.

Thanks are also extended to David Upton for his work on editing and proof-reading.

The authors would like to express their gratitude to the sponsors of the study: the Arts Council of England, Association for Business Sponsorship of the Arts, Calouste Gulbenkian Foundation, Comino Foundation, the CLEA (Council for Local Education Authorities) Annual Research Programme, Crayola Ltd., and Powys LEA.

Finally, the authors would like to thank the RSA for commissioning this project.

The effects and effectiveness of arts education in schools

Commissioned by the Royal Society for the encouragement of Arts, Manufactures & Commerce

INTERIM REPORT 1

John Harland
Kay Kinder
Jo Haynes
Ian Schagen

Published in October 1998
by the National Foundation for Educational Research,
The Mere, Upton Park, Slough, Berkshire SL1 2DQ

ISBN 0 7005 8

1. THE STUDY

BACKGROUND

The UK research literature on the effects of arts education and the nature of the teaching practices and schools' policies that may give rise to these effects is not very extensive. Although valuable evaluations of individual arts projects and initiatives in schools have been undertaken, they have tended to focus on processes rather than outcomes and have rarely examined the cumulative effects of involvement in school-based arts education. The absence of a comprehensive and empirically based theoretical framework for conceptualising such effects is particularly noticeable.

In order to redress the shortage of studies in this area and explore the potential implications for policy and practice, the RSA (Royal Society for the encouragement of Arts, Manufactures & Commerce) has launched an independent research project as part of its programme called 'The Arts Matter'. The National Foundation for Educational Research (NFER) has been commissioned to conduct the research. The study, which is scheduled to last for three years, started in the spring of 1997. It is co-funded by the Arts Council of England, Assocation for Business Sponsorship of the Arts, Calouste Gulbenkian Foundation, Comino Foundation, the CLEA (Council for Local Education Authorities) Annual Research Programme, Crayola Ltd., and Powys LEA.

AIMS

The project has four main aims:

(i)   to document and evidence the range of effects and outcomes attributable to school-based arts education;

(ii)   to examine the relationship between these effects and the key factors and processes associated with arts provision in schools;

(iii)   to illuminate good practice in schools' provision of high-quality educational experiences in the arts; and

(iv)   to study the extent to which high levels of institutional involvement in the arts correlate with the qualities known to be associated with successful school improvement and school effectiveness.

Using data collected during the initial year of the project (Phase 1), this interim report attempts to fulfil the first of these aims by offering a typology of the outcomes of schools-based arts education for discussion and subsequent refinement. Once this has been achieved, later reports will examine the project's other objectives, particularly how the achievement of these effects may relate to the practices and processes associated with arts teaching and learning in the schools. Further details about the full project are set out in Appendix I.

METHODS

The evidence for this analysis was collected through case study fieldwork in five secondary schools with a reputation for good practice in the arts. Following a lengthy period of information-gathering and consultations, five schools in different LEAs agreed to participate in this longitudinal part of the study. The sample provides a variety of institutions and settings (e.g. urban and rural schools, schools of different sizes, a range of contrasting socio-economic contexts, a GMS school, and schools in LEAs renowned for their strong support for the arts). Equally, within each institution, a range of organisational structures for arts teaching (e.g. faculty versus departments) has emerged, as well as some interesting variation in the perceived strengths and public reputation of different artforms.

Throughout 1997, the research team spent the equivalent of eight fieldwork days in each of the case study schools. These days were used to:

- observe arts subjects being taught, followed by short post-observation interviews with teachers and pupils;
- interview eight Year 7 and eight Year 9 pupils in each school;
- conduct interviews and have informal meetings with headteachers, heads of department/faculty, arts teachers, and, in some schools, LEA arts advisory staff and community arts workers;
- conduct short interviews with teachers of subjects other than the arts; and
- pilot a Year 11 questionnaire with samples of Year 11 pupils for use in Phase 2 of the project.

The Year 7 and 9 pupil samples were selected by asking teachers of art, dance, drama and music to nominate pupils who were making good progress in at least one of the artforms. This sampling strategy was considered consistent with the emphasis in the case study element of the project on investigating practices that were deemed to be effective. In practice, however, it should be noted that pupils who were enthusiastic and positive about one artform did not necessarily feel the same about the others.

The staff sample was chosen in consultation with the headteacher or a member of the senior management team. They defined what the 'arts' encompassed within their schools and recommended teacher representatives of each of the included artforms, as well as appropriate members of senior management (e.g. deputy heads with responsibility for the curriculum or pastoral support). In all five schools, at least one teacher or head of department for art, drama and music was interviewed – very often two teachers of these subjects were interviewed. In three schools, dance was included in the 'arts' domain and, hence, an interview was held with the dance teacher. In the fourth school, dance was not considered to be taught as part of the arts, though one of the drama teachers interviewed taught some 'dance-drama' within drama; the teacher who taught dance as a component of PE was interviewed as one of the sample of teachers of non-arts subjects. In the fifth school, dance was not taught to any significant degree, though one of the drama teachers reported teaching '*some basic dance skills*' as part of mime in drama. The heads of English were interviewed in the three schools where the headteachers believed that the school's implementation of this subject shared affinities with arts-oriented subjects.

In all, 52 full and recorded interviews were conducted with 48 interviewees including arts teachers, heads of department, school senior managers and LEA personnel. Broken down, this sample comprised two LEA arts advisers, five headteachers, nine deputies, three members of staff in other senior positions, 17 heads of department and 12 teachers of arts subjects. It can be seen that 17 of this sample held senior management posts in schools, though seven of these had a background in the teaching of the arts (including English).

Data from these sources have been used to construct a typology of teachers' perceptions of the aims and effects of arts education (see Chapter 2) and to portray pupils' perspectives on the same topic (see Chapter 4). The report also includes a presentation of the results of a secondary analysis of information on input and outcome scores for school-leaver cohorts collected by NFER's 'Quantitative Analysis for Self-Evaluation' (QUASE) project. These analyses, whilst unable to establish causality, explore the possible relationships between the taking of arts-oriented GCSE courses and general academic achievement at GCSE (see Chapter 5).

It should be stressed that the report in its entirety is an interim working paper, the purpose of which is limited to that of offering some provisional findings for consideration and discussion. At this early stage in the project, no attempt is being made to reach definitive and confident conclusions. Instead, the report aspires only to contribute to the current debate by presenting some tentative new findings which need to be refined and developed, by identifying issues and methodological options to inform further research, and, perhaps, by suggesting ways some of the arguments about arts education could be progressed.

2. TEACHERS' PERCEPTIONS OF
THE EFFECTS OF ARTS EDUCATION

INTRODUCTION

By way of embarking on the analysis required to meet the study's first aim, this opening chapter presents a provisional and tentative typology of the possible effects of school-based arts education, as seen by teachers and heads of department of arts-oriented subjects, and members of senior management. All these interviewees were specifically asked to identify what they saw as the key effects or outcomes of their particular arts subject or, if more appropriate, the arts in general. Many also volunteered descriptions of effects in response to other questions in the interview schedule. The typology was constructed by carefully trawling through the 52 staff interviews in the five case study schools and recording all references to claims about the effects, desirable outcomes and achievable aims associated with arts subjects (for the sake of brevity, these terms are used interchangeably throughout this chapter).

Given that teachers could be said to have a natural vested interest in accentuating the positive benefits to be gained through involvement in the arts, their perceptions of the outcomes of arts education have been treated as 'claims' that require empirical verification. Although this approach has the disadvantage of underestimating the significance of a majority of teachers independently citing similar arts-related outcomes, it offers the crucial advantage of encouraging the search for valid and rigorous evidence to corroborate or refute teachers' accounts.

It is also important to stress that all the categories in the typology were created on the basis of what was found in the interview transcripts – that is to say, a bottom-up or empirically grounded approach to the framing of the categories was used. Emphatically, they were not constructed in any *a priori* manner whereby the constructs are established in advance by the researchers and laid on the data like a template, either at the interview stage or in the analysis. The only slight exception to this was, in the later phases of the analysis, the transferring of one category or sub-category from one artform (including the arts collectively) to another for comparative purposes.

When considering the typology, it is essential to bear in mind that each of the presented categories represents an ideal type that has been somewhat artificially singled out as a discrete entity in order to assist analyses and inform discussions about policies and practices in the teaching of the arts. These advantages, however, are only achieved through a process of fragmentation which inevitably sacrifices a sense of the holistic nature of an individual's experiences in the arts. Consequently, in later analyses, it will be necessary to inquire how these categories relate to one another, when looked at from the perspective of individual experiences and biographies. For example, it will be interesting to explore whether arts experiences in their entirety are greater than the sum of the individual parts or categories described in the typology below. For present purposes, suffice it to acknowledge that, in reality, several of the categories often overlapped with each other and that many of the references identified in the interview material contained allusions to more than one category. For such observations, a system of cross-referencing and multiple coding was applied.

A three-tiered classification system was developed to categorise and group teachers' perceptions of the effects of arts education. A diagrammatic overview of the typology is set out in Figures 1-4.

A TYPOLOGY OF CLAIMED EFFECTS

Four broad types of purported effects were evident in teachers' accounts:

A.   Effects on pupils
B.   Effects on the school
C.   Effects on the community
D.   Art itself as an outcome

Unsurprisingly, the first of these – claimed effects on pupils – was by far the largest broad type. Within it, 12 main categories were identified. Most of these contain distinct sub-categories. Two of the main categories (Categories 1 and 4) contain sub-categories which relate to individual artforms, while the remainder denote effects (in theory at least) that may be generated by all the artforms or the arts in general. The first three of the main categories are primarily concerned with the development of different forms of knowledge and understanding.

Figure 1

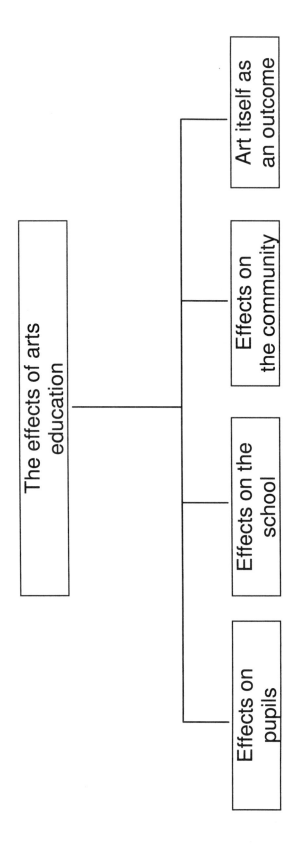

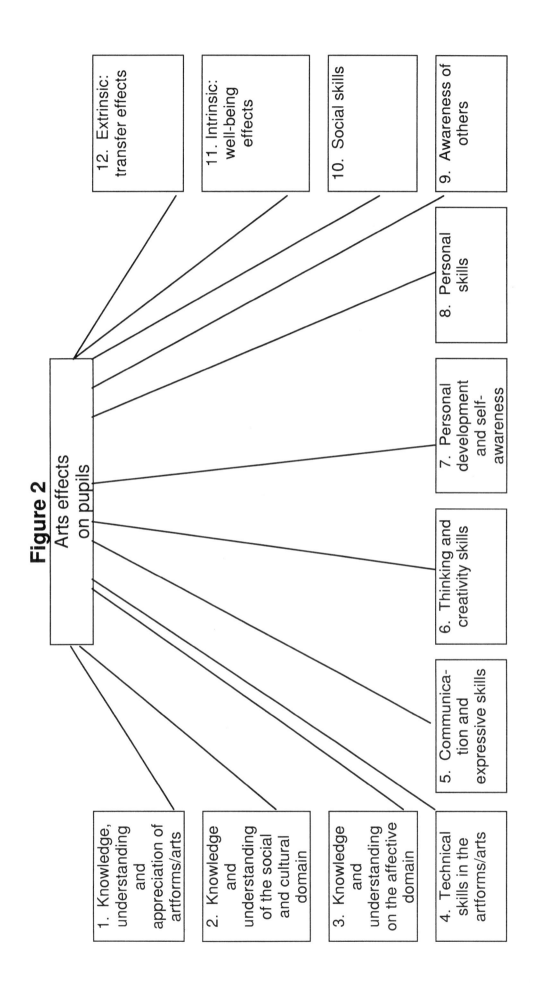

Figure 2

Arts effects on pupils

1. Knowledge, understanding and appreciation of artforms/arts

2. Knowledge and understanding of the social and cultural domain

3. Knowledge and understanding on the affective domain

4. Technical skills in the artforms/arts

5. Communication and expressive skills

6. Thinking and creativity skills

7. Personal development and self-awareness

8. Personal skills

9. Awareness of others

10. Social skills

11. Intrinsic: well-being effects

12. Extrinsic: transfer effects

Figure 3

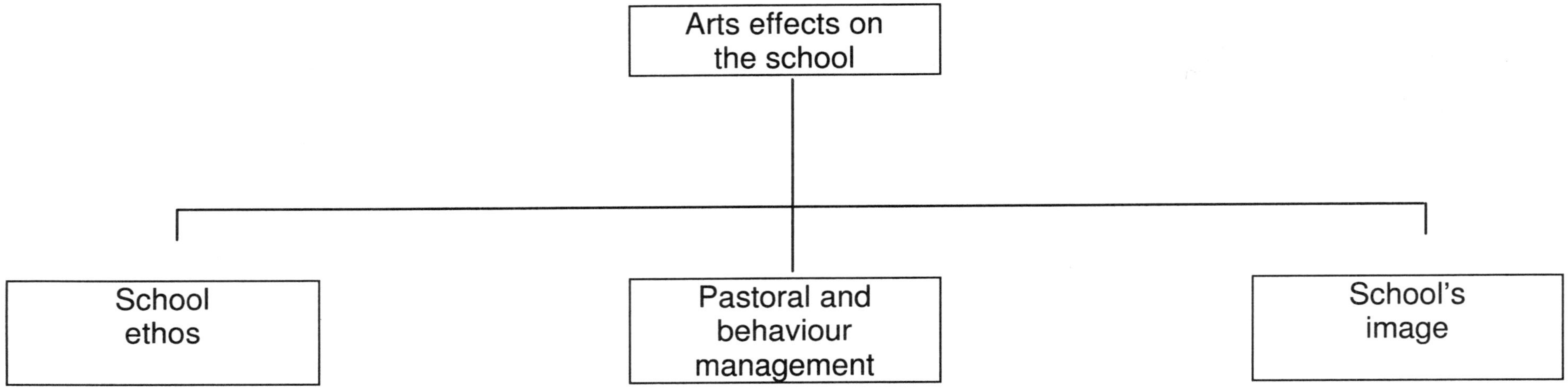

```
                    ┌──────────────┐
                    │ Arts effects │
                    │   on the     │
                    │   school     │
                    └──────┬───────┘
        ┌──────────────────┼──────────────────┐
        │                  │                  │
┌───────────────┐  ┌───────────────┐  ┌───────────────┐
│    School      │  │  Pastoral and │  │   School's    │
│    ethos       │  │   behaviour   │  │    image      │
│                │  │  management   │  │               │
└───────────────┘  └───────────────┘  └───────────────┘
```

Figure 4

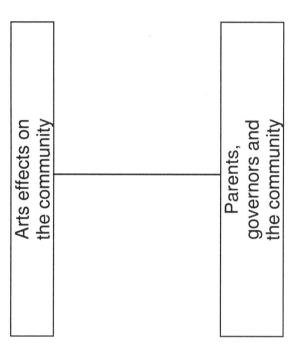

A. EFFECTS ON PUPILS

1.0 *CLAIMS ABOUT EFFECTS RELATING TO INCREASES IN KNOWLEDGE, UNDERSTANDING AND APPRECIATION OF THE ARTS AND INDIVIDUAL ARTFORMS*

This category covers claims pertaining to developments in pupils' knowledge and values about the arts themselves, either as individual artforms or as a collective entity. The category is divided into eight sub-categories: the first five relate in turn to each of the artforms (i.e. art, dance, drama, English and music), while the final three deal with increased levels of appreciation of and motivation towards the arts in general.

1.1 (a) Increases knowledge and understanding of paintings/works of *VISUAL ART*, critical study skills, language to discuss art, in general and unspecified ways.

One contribution from a teacher captured much of the character of this potential outcome:

> *I am hoping that they have got a greater awareness of art heritage, history of art, plus I always try to get them to look at things and say 'Well, do you think it is good, even if you don't like it?' when we are looking at a work of art. Like 'Why has Picasso done this face like this when he can really draw like this?'. I hope that by the end of it, they have a little bit more understanding of art and that it's not just painting a pretty picture and why artists work the way that they do* (art teacher).

Descriptions of the purported effects in this sub-category highlighted how the increased use of '*investigations*', '*research projects*', '*evaluations*' and classroom displays had led to extensions in pupils' '*knowledge of critical and contextual implications*' of artists' work. It was observed that the growth in outcomes associated with 'critical studies' had been nurtured by the National Curriculum for art and the pioneering work of some LEAs in this area. Some art teachers drew attention to the importance of equipping young people with a language to discuss, interpret and evaluate works of art:

> *And you're giving them a specialist arts vocabulary, just by using it all the time in the lesson and they're picking it up and they can then apply it informally ... they discuss each other's work informally. They will even assess each other's work – 'Oh, that handle doesn't look quite right' – or whatever.*

(b) Develops ability to read a painting or read an image and understand it.

While the first sub-category is intended to denote effects associated with the development of critical study skills at a general level, this sub-category refers specifically to the growth in capacities to interpret or 'decode' particular works of art. One teacher expressed the point succinctly:

I am trying to show them that the work of a particular artist is not solely the end product, it is the thinking behind it and the exploration and how they have arrived at that. To do that, you have got to look deeper than just the actual superficial thing that is hanging on the wall at the end (ex head of art).

(c) Extends appreciation of the visual artform, develops aesthetic judgement-making.

Comments in this sub-category were comparatively frequent and they focused on the development of aesthetic judgements through widening pupils' experience, awareness and appreciation of the visual arts. Typical contributions from three different art teachers were:

They have fairly fixed, traditional ideas about what they think good art is and what they think bad art is, so it is breaking down the prejudices as far as they are concerned.

Sometimes they would say 'I don't think that is as good as that' and you say 'Why not?' and they say 'Because that is messy and that is actually beautifully drawn', and then you can go into 'Well you know there are reasons why that is good and that isn't'... I think that they absorb such a lot.

I try to get them to have that love of looking at works of art.

(d) Increases knowledge and understanding of historical context of visual art.

There were no further and more detailed references to this sub-category of outcomes, beyond those alluded to already (e.g. history of art in 1.1a).

1.2   (a) Increases knowledge and understanding of *DANCE*, critical study skills, language to discuss dance, in unspecified ways.

Perhaps indicating an interesting difference between the teaching of dance and other artforms in the secondary school curriculum, there was only one reference that fell within this sub-category. The fostering of the capacity to appraise others' work was mentioned by a dance teacher:

From a dance perspective, ... developing ... an appreciation of composition, performance, analysing others, the ability to evaluate, would all come within that.

The lack of any other references here may suggest that the 'critical studies' approach in dance is less evident than in other arts-oriented subjects. If so, this carries important implications for how the effectiveness of dance teaching should be judged.

(b) Develops ability to view a dance performance and understand it.
There were no further references to this type of outcome beyond the comment made in 1.2a.

(c) Extends appreciation of the dance artform, develops aesthetic judgement-making.
Only one interviewee offered a comment which was vaguely relevant to this sub-category. In contrast to the corresponding contributions for the visual arts (see 1.1c), which were specifically concerned with enhancing aesthetic judgement-making, the following comment is limited to promoting awareness and appreciation only in the most general of senses:

> *The main objective was to make people more aware, make people more aware of dance in its own right ... [The outcomes are] ... more awareness primarily, hopefully more understanding of where they sit, not literally, but where they are within the world of the arts: whether or not they feel that their own involvement is perhaps going to the theatre, opening their eyes to productions and performances out of school, or whether or not that is something that they actually feel that they want to take away and they want to improve and they want to develop within themselves* (dance and PE teacher).

However, it is important to recognise here that dance as an artform has a much more precarious status in the curriculum than the other main artforms. As this interviewee went on to argue, it can be an outcome itself to get pupils to appreciate that dance is an artform, not merely '*a PE activity*':

> *The biggest thing that I want to get through is allowing every pupil ... the ability to develop movement potential; develop an appreciation of the artform, in that way; develop dance not as a PE activity, but as an activity that develops in its own right as complementary to other artforms. So that is my main objective* (dance and PE teacher).

(d) Increases knowledge and understanding of historical context of dance.
There were no significant claims made about such effects for dance.

1.3 (a) Increases knowledge and understanding of *DRAMA*, theatre/plays, critical study skills, language to discuss dramatic artform, in unspecified ways.
Drama teachers talked about their subject extending pupils' 'critical faculties' and making them '*more discerning, more discriminating*'. For some, the application of these faculties to television was an important outcome:

> *Also, there is the aesthetic side to it as well, you want them to appreciate what is good practice. I mean there is a skills side to drama as well and you try to open their eyes to things which are right, true ... one of the things that kids do all the time these days is sit in front of the television and I honestly feel that*

drama enhances that experience. If they are going to do that, sit in front of the television, I think they might as well do it with some sort of discernment and I think that drama can teach that sort of thing. I get feedback from pupils all the time on that; they are beginning to realise that some things are dross and some things are really quite good, for certain reasons. They are more able to articulate the reasons that things are good and so I think that it can help them make better use of their leisure time, to not be couch potatoes, but to be discriminating.

The critical review and evaluation of work created by themselves and others was also mentioned. Other teachers cited the appreciation of theatrical form as an outcome, especially at key stage 4.

(b) Develops ability to read/see a play and understand it.

More specifically than 1.3a, one drama teacher described this effect in the following way:

Then it is the sense of achievement when it works and the sense of achievement, for example, when we had a theatre company come in and the Year 7s who saw it would have understood. They did quite a subtle technique at the beginning, used a subtle style, and they can understand it. And they can use subject-specific words and that's good, that's clever, you know, they understand that, so there's a real boost there ...

A headteacher argued that this capacity to understand plays, once developed, will last into adult life.

(c) Extends appreciation of the theatrical artform, develops aesthetic judgement-making.

One interviewee expressed this type of outcome as an aim: '*I want them to have an appreciation and to be able to be analytical about the things that they come across in terms of drama.*' One drama teacher's reference to the claimed effect of making pupils more discerning and discriminating has already been given, especially with regard to television (see 1.3a). Another drama teacher in a different school also attempted to engender an aesthetic sense through television drama:

I tend to start with television because that is what they know, isn't it? That is their form of theatre. When they do go to the theatre, they are constantly blown away ... and they are so impressed by everything, by the seats ... the aesthetic tends to be learnt from school productions, and the appreciation of drama like that. In key stage 4, when they go out to the theatre and see other experts, they appreciate [the form].

In addition, a music teacher pointed to the effect of encouraging pupils to appreciate drama and theatre as an artform.

13

(d) Increases knowledge and understanding of historical context of theatre.

There were no significant claims made about such effects for drama.

1.4   (a) Increases knowledge and understanding of *ENGLISH*, critical study skills, language to discuss literature, in unspecified ways.

Given its traditional role and high status within the teaching of English, this effect was often taken for granted by the departmental heads interviewed in the first phase; instead, they tended to focus on the creative 'making' dimension to the subject. Some heads of English, however, did refer to it explicitly as a very significant effect:

> *I also think that it is very important to make them into a critical audience when it comes to literature.*

> [discussing the reading and commenting on each others' work] *They are capable of doing it and that immediate feedback, critical response to your own work, then enables you to go on and say 'Well right, you just looked at that from your friend' or 'You have just written your own analysis and evaluation of what you did; now here is something else to look at. What do you think of that?'*

It is tempting to speculate whether the tendency for English teachers to see creativity as the connecting point with arts-oriented subjects indicates that, to some extent, they (and teachers of other subjects) fail to recognise that arts teachers share a common concern with the teaching of critical skills, evaluation and review. If so, do opportunities for joint reflection, if not cross-curriculum initiatives, go begging?

(b) Develops ability to read a piece of literature and understand it, demystifies it.

One head of English focused on the demystification element of this sub-category:

> *It is about breaking the myths down about literature and encouraging them to have their own personal response to literature – very, very important. Giving them the confidence to be able to say 'Well I disagree with that' or 'I don't like that' or 'I think that is badly done, badly written'. To actually feel that simply because it is written on a piece of paper doesn't mean that that is absolute, you know, perfection.*

Another head of English definitely linked the development of the competence to critically analyse and understand works of literature to pupils engaging in the processes of creative composition by understanding literature '*from the inside*':

> *In terms of literature, it helps them to understand what literature is about by doing it themselves and by having to hone, that they know what – one labours the terms like similes and metaphors – but you hope eventually that they get the idea that the use of analogy is one of the main creative tools, that we describe one thing by another and that one hopes that they'll start to*

understand literature from the inside ... and to have understood it from the inside, that by doing it yourself, you understand it better, so that one hopes that when they come in in Year 7 and they write trite four-lined quatrains that make no sense, that by the end of Year 7, hopefully, they've understood that poetry isn't just producing a lot of nonsense that rhymes, but that it's about expressing with originality and insight and careful choice of language, what it is that one is attempting to – what one sees in the world and what one wants to say.

(c) Extends appreciation of literature as a artform, develops aesthetic judgement-making.

Over and above the earlier extract on the development of personal responses to literature, there was only one other comment relevant to this sub-category and it was made by the same head of English:

I hope that they will leave with a love of the arts and that they will continue to follow that through in all sorts of different ways. That they won't be afraid to go and see a play ... and that they will go away independent and inquisitive readers.

(d) Increases knowledge and understanding of historical context of literature.

There were no significant claims made about such effects for English.

1.5   (a) Increases knowledge and understanding of *MUSIC*, critical study skills, language to discuss music, in unspecified ways.

There was only one general reference identified as belonging to this category: the development of critical skills.

(b) Develops ability to listen to a piece of music and understand it.

One headteacher emphasised the effect of valuing, listening to and appreciating the work of fellow pupils. Similarly, a head of music stressed that the achievement of the aim of encouraging the enjoyment of music was dependent on enhancing young people's capacity to listen to and understand particular pieces: '*When they know more about the type of music that they are listening to, they sort of understand it more and they tolerate it.*' Another accentuated the analytical side of listening to music. Clearly, this outcome is also closely related to the development of auditory skills and abilities (see 4.6), though here the focus is on increases in knowledge about the musical form and its contextual circumstances (see 1.5d below).

(c) Extends appreciation of music as an artform, develops aesthetic judgement-making.

The appreciation of music was cited as an effect, though, interestingly, generally without the references to the development of critical and aesthetic judgement-making evident in art and drama, for example:

> *Basically to provide pupils with an understanding of what's gone before them, so to have an awareness of the culture within music, so at the end of the day, even if they don't do any playing in school at all and they don't perform in any shows, musicals, they don't do any dance, that they go away being able to appreciate music* (head of music).

In one school, where the music department had worked very hard at demonstrating to pupils that music at school could incorporate student's own musical preferences and styles, there was the recognition that in order to extend pupils' appreciation of music, teachers needed to show first that they could appreciate the music pupils brought with them to school. Consequently, a perceived effect was the dismantling of the perception that school music equated with classical or traditional music:

> *We seem to have broken the barrier in school, that music is a cool thing to do, music is a cool place to hang out ...* (music teacher).

(d) Increases knowledge and understanding of historical context of music.

There were no significant claims made about such effects for music.

1.6 Fosters perceptions of cross-arts continuities and differences.

For some interviewees, the effects of engaging in several artforms or participating in integrated arts programmes could be greater than the sum of the individual artform parts. This is a potentially very significant point for the research and one that will need to be borne in mind when considering the effectiveness of teaching and learning in the arts. Are certain outcomes most attainable through, if not dependent on, pupils taking several different artform programmes or some type of integrated or cross-arts projects? This music teacher appeared to think so:

> *I think that we get a lot of pupils, I think, in here that are immersed, very much, in the arts; they don't just specialise. We do get a lot of ... crossing between the two or between the three and because of that I really do think that they become very individual. We do get pupils more individual and they do pick up certain subjects specifically, but I think if you talk about what the arts are doing for the pupils as people, not just knowledge-wise, actually doing for them as people, it very much crosses across all through* [the arts].

The following is an example of the kind of project that was seen as offering such effects:

> *Then the whole thing became such a synthesis of ideas. Me and [x] put ideas forward and then we got some of the other pupils composing some computer*

music. We set up a couple of computers in there that were running continuous loops. Then we actually set speakers under the audience so that it was running their music as the play was going on. It became such an absolute ... I remember sitting back and thinking 'This is such a brilliant synthesis of all the arts; if you could video this and package this you could sell this to anybody who wants to come in and say what does arts do in school and how does it come in from the community?' It started off with this sort of strange play that they were reading and it became something so completely different in many ways (music teacher).

A head of music maintained that the effect of nurturing cross-artform perceptions was better achieved through a department rather than a faculty structure:

It enables them to see [links across the arts] *... in order to see the links between artforms, which we feel are important, and hence our collaborative approach at certain times. In order to see those links, kids have got to see the differences and appreciate the difference between a performing subject like drama or discussing and performing, a performing and listening subject like music, a practical hands-on subject like art or sculpting – whatever – the more physical side of dance and so on. If they are to begin to understand the commonality, the themes, the themes of approaches, perceptions within those subjects, they have got to see the differences first.*

A drama teacher in another school (with an arts faculty) also emphasised the value of perceiving the differences, as well the similarities between different artforms:

So I think an arts faculty has to work very, very hard for the shared experience, whilst really appreciating the differences.

1.7   Extends appreciation of the arts.
This sub-category was used to collate references to the impact of the arts in general on artistic discernment, aesthetic judgement and the encouragement of positive attitudes towards the arts. Such effects were variously described:

When you think that we have pupils who have left here now, who have seen an artist in residence; they have been out, they have worked on sculptures, out in the car park. I mean ten years ago they would have walked the other way or thrown a brick at it probably [laughter]. *No, that is an exaggeration, but that sort of transformation of appreciation of others, of the arts* (deputy head, i/c pastoral).

I think what's gained is that pupils, again it's an appreciation, it's not just a mechanical thing of drawing, as it's not just a mechanical thing of composing. We teach them how to appreciate pieces of artwork, whether it be music or drama, and I think it would be quite nice to get that into the curriculum; you know, appreciation of art ... the appreciation, which really is one of the most important things (head of music).

For an adviser, encouraging appreciation of the arts inevitably entailed giving young people access to the arts and artists, both as audience members and by creating themselves:

> *Unless we as teachers and advisory teachers can help them to understand the conventions of dance [for example], of how dance actually works, then they have no way of entering into it. It is literally a closed book to them; they can't read it. Consequently, I suspect they may be turned off it, until they can come at it in a different way. So, it is trying to create, through the understanding of the various artforms, a way in which youngsters can be receptive to those artforms, so they can actually make meaning from them, they can actually enter them ... by talking to artists, by interviewing artists, by having works mediated for them by experts. The youngsters can enter in the discourse, they can see what is going on, they can understand what the artist was trying to do. Of course, once you can begin to do that, it becomes part of you, it becomes part of your own artistic endeavour, but at the same time allows you then ... it opens up the whole world of the arts, it gives you that, it gives you an access to artforms.*

Several teachers independently recounted how when teachers and pupils work together in a creative enterprise, a certain moment can sometimes occur when all the participants instinctively know that whatever it is they are producing could not be bettered. This aesthetic experiential sense was described as acquiring a form of artistic appreciation when things are right:

> *That there is an appreciation of what good arts practice is about, when you have that moment when you just know it couldn't be better, the kids know it and you know it, that something really good has happened* (deputy head i/c curriculum).

Hence, it is the appreciation of the aesthetic, as well as the arts, which is the purported outcome. This point is taken up by a drama teacher, when describing the impact s/he is attempting to achieve:

> *If you like, to open up their soul and find out what is in it. That is what I am looking to do in teaching arts subjects: to get them to look deeper than the surface and find out what is really underneath and to appreciate things that are good, and to quote Keats, good and beautiful.*

Other interviewees talked about the claimed effect of developing an aesthetic awareness. An art teacher, for example, saw the fostering of a general aesthetic sense as a key outcome of an 'arts' education:

> *Recognising, I like to think, good design, appreciating architecture, film, anything like that and without a decent arts education you are not going to do that.*

And from a head of a department for Welsh:

[The arts] *give children an appreciation and an understanding of what is valuable, other than making money if you like, because very often it's difficult to – it gives people an understanding of aesthetic work, aesthetic value, or what the value of the aesthetic [is].*

1.8 Encourages sense of inspiration/motivation in the artform, higher aspirations, hard-working approach, determination, sense of purpose.

The final sub-category in the first of the main categories extends the notions of knowledge, understanding and appreciation of the arts to the claimed consequential effect (for some pupils) of increased motivation and inspiration. In the words of one interviewee, pupils can become '*fired up*'; words like 'inspiration', 'interest' and 'involvement' as outcomes were volunteered by many teachers. For example, an art teacher remarked:

> *I think that arts education means a lot to me because I can see the influence over 28 years that I have had on different girls. The commitment, motivation, enthusiasm and skill that can be brought out of people.*

Several teachers pointed to the effect of pupils being inspired to achieve higher standards rather than accept just satisfactory levels of performance. Raising aspirations was seen as a necessary outcome prior to attaining higher levels of achievement. Others described it as the promotion of a positive and ambitious '*can do*' mentality in the arts. In English, the motivation to want to write better and effectively was seen as revolving around '*a love of the creative power of language*'. Furthermore, a deputy head described the arts' impact in terms of the constant drive to improve and reach higher:

> *In art, they say 'Well yes, this is interesting, you are working well here, have you thought about ...?' So, it is not 'That's good, fine, it's finished' – it is about the working on, working to improve whatever you have got.*

As well as inspiring individuals, a deputy head underlined the importance of having an impact on peer group cultures, if young people are to be able to engage enthusiastically in the arts without the ridicule and censure of their friends:

> *They do take part in leisure activities that directly relate to the arts now; we are talking about 13-year-olds who will go away and be a member of an art club. It is not frowned upon now. That is so important for kids of this age: if anything has not got the street cred or makes you look a swat, or whatever today's word is, yes that is right. If being an artist, or having art in your bedroom when your friends come around, or having anything like that, doesn't have that, 'Oh well, I am not going to take them upstairs because that is where I have been doing this work.' If people have the confidence to be like that now at 13, that is the important thing; if it is cool it is ... and it is. I would never have thought that transformation could have taken place in [X], but it has.*

This observation echoes the earlier comment on the way in which changes have been brought about so that '*music is a cool place to hang out*' (see 1.5c).

2.0 ***CLAIMS ABOUT EF[...] [...]G TO INCREASES IN KNOWLEDGE AND [...] THE SOCIAL AND CULTURAL DOMAIN***

This category moves on from the clai[...] [...]sed knowledge, understanding and appreciation of the arts themselves to po[...] [...]e extensions in knowledge and understanding about different social and cultural contexts that may be achieved through studying arts-oriented subjects. It contains three sub-categories, all of which can include references to the individual artforms and the arts in general.

2.1 Develops awareness, understanding, knowledge of cultural traditions (e.g. brass bands, Welsh poetry), raising or broadening child's cultural diversity/perspective/horizons, multicultural insights/benefits.

All of the artforms were posited as impacting positively on young people's cultural perspectives and awareness. Music, for example, was seen as enriching the lives of pupils who played in bands and travelled widely abroad; drama attempted to broaden cultural horizons through theatre trips and widen the horizons beyond television; English encouraged the capacity to see things from a different perspective; and the '*use of the work of other artists* [in art] *and reference to the context in which art was produced* [develops] *an awareness of the art of cultures other than our own*'; and '*if nothing else,* [dance] *has educated them in what other people do, different styles, different lifestyles, different cultures, history, you know*'.

In particular, the arts were considered to have an important role to perform in shaping attitudes in a multiethnic and multicultural society – both in schools with high proportions of children from the ethnic minorities and those with very low proportions:

> *One of our objectives is to use the arts as a way of enhancing our youngsters' appreciation of cultural diversity. I think in a predominantly white school that is a strong objective that you find ways of doing it. We linked with a school in central Birmingham, our India link ... we have very strongly embraced things that access us to other cultures and the arts is often the way that different cultures communicate to each other most easily* (head).

In schools with a high ratio of ethnic minority children, the arts were seen as offering an opportunity for pupils to explore their own cultures and cultural identity, as well as providing a means of sharing and incorporating the different cultures that exist within a school. They also permitted the fostering of insights into 'high' and 'low' or popular cultural forms.

2.2 Promotes awareness and perceptions of pupils' surroundings and their place within them.

This perceived effect was particularly prevalent in the visual arts, such was the force and frequency of many art teachers' exhortation to really 'look' at the world as it really is:

I suppose in essence what we are trying to do is to sensitise individuals to their environment and to their surroundings, things that they see, touch and experience (ex head of art).

This is a very obvious thing to all art teachers, you can put a whole lot of white things together on a table – white cloth and white objects – and you can say 'What colour are they?' They all say 'White'; then you say 'What colour is this white compared to that white?' And they will say 'Oh, that is darker, but that really isn't white anymore; it is maybe grey, maybe bluish,' And they go 'Oh yes', you know, it is like it is there all the time but they need to be shown these things. I think that we have an awareness that we can pass on to other people that makes them go like that ... I think there is a lot of that sort of thing in teaching people to really look at things (head of expressive arts).

We work from direct observation so it makes them study and be aware of everything that's around them ... (ceramics teacher).

Seventy-five/80 per cent of all our sense skills comes through our eyes, and yet for much of the time we use our eyes as radar, just to stop us knocking into things. Yet, there is this exciting world that we live in, that even if they never looked at another painting again, you know the colours of the trees, the sky, the change of light, the effect of light on structures, pattern, texture, all those things that we talk about art and all around them. If just a kid can say 'Hey, look at the colour in that leaf Mr [X]', even though they are just doing it to please me, that is great, but I would hope that some of that holds.

This type of outcome, however, was not completely limited to the visual arts, as teachers of other artforms demonstrated. Drama was viewed as '*a means of really looking at the world and making their own decisions about it*'. English, according to one head of department, should lead to '*an awareness that in literature there are important insights about the world that they live in*'.

Additionally, there were several testimonies to the power of the arts in general to inform an awareness of the world, to help young people make sense of their world and work out where they stand within it:

The arts are the way in which children can be offered the opportunity of looking ... of responding to their world and making statements about their world – whether it is music, language, literature, fine art – and that for me is the strength for the arts (head).

I think that again, art involvement, I think for teenagers is particularly important, because I think in those years you're learning quite often to make your way in the world and to do that you have to communicate with it, yes, and to understand it, interpret it; and the creative and expressive arts allow, or provide, teenagers with an opportunity, an added opportunity other than just language (head of Welsh).

2.3 Fosters awareness and exploration of social and moral issues, social life, society, racial awareness, human rights.

Drama and English were particularly associated with this perceived effect. Most of the drama teachers alluded to this type of impact, citing the exploration of social issues, such as racism, as a significant contribution to the pupils' social and moral education:

> *One of the things that you really try to do in drama is give a wider understanding of society as a whole.*

> [talking about the effects of drama] *You're educating in the arts, you're educating towards a better understanding of what life is like and a bit more of an idea of how groups of people can organise things and change things and develop things through the simulated activity of drama. So they're learning about life.*

English too was attributed with a similar capacity to attune young people to fundamental social and moral issues:

> *We've just finished reading* To Kill a Mocking Bird *– Harper Lee – and I think that that is a very civilising work for young people to read: civilising in the sense that it's morally enlightening without being overtly didactic. I would want to open children's minds to the power of language, the civilising power of the creative mind, attempting to encompass the beauty of the world, the sadness of the world, so I see it as a humanising discipline* (head of English).

Other artforms were also deemed to have this 'humanising' potential. Endorsing the findings of other studies based on classroom observations of art lessons, one art teacher described something of the quality of discussions of social issues that can occur during sessions when a group is engaged in an absorbing practical activity:

> *Well, if it was weddings, it might be to do with arranged marriages, it might be divorce, what it is like just living with a mum, how old you should be when you get married. There is just a lot and I think that given the right atmosphere in the classroom, which of course is up to the teacher to generate, and everyone on task, in an art lesson, you can be working and having a whole group discussion at the same time. On perfect occasions, which happens sometimes, where everyone is quietly working, you can have 25 people in the room at once working and you can have conversations with the group at once. I think that is the nicest time really, when it is like that.*

3.0 CLAIMS ABOUT EFFECTS RELATING TO INCREASES IN KNOWLEDGE AND UNDERSTANDING OF THE AFFECTIVE DOMAIN

The third of the main categories is contained within a single sub-category.

3.1 Develops an understanding/heightened awareness of the world of feelings, emotions, mood, spirituality.

Claims entered under this sub-category centred on the increased understanding of pupils' own emotions and spirituality, and those of others – it represents a growth in what others have called 'emotional intelligence'. One headteacher expressed this outcome when commenting on the process of internalisation that the arts can precipitate:

> *That internalising helps them to understand themselves, their own feelings, because I don't think we have mentioned that much, their feelings about the world and the way in which they can make statements that are aggressive statements, or sensitive statements or whatever, but they can do that through the art experience. People talk about drama being a way of directing anger and understanding relationships and tensions between two people through that drama. So it is to do with the sense and the feelings, and the spirit.*

Drama was often depicted as an important carrier-subject for this particular type of effect. Recognising the outward behavioural signals of people's moods and emotional states was considered to be an important step towards engendering an increased awareness of other people's inner states of mind:

> *Just a very simple introduction to mime is always, you know, 'Mould me into a teacher at the front of the class who is very angry but isn't saying anything.' You know, and they'll then become aware of 'Gosh, yes, we do know when we are giving off signals.' You know, 'Mould yourself into someone who is madly in love and is trying to hide it.' You know what I mean, looking at those subtle differences, you know, we're very fascinating animals, so, you know, we've got to live with each other, work and play with each other, so how do we understand each other?* (drama teacher).

It would be wrong, however, to give the impression that such outcomes were the sole preserve of drama; interviewees testified to other artforms producing similar effects. Two deputy heads, neither of whom taught arts-oriented subjects, spoke of the effects they had observed in pupils:

> *You are talking about relationships and emotion, aren't you? If you had ever been to any of our concerts or our productions, by golly you would feel it then. You do see it; it is there the difference that it makes to people.*

> *That greater appreciation, that greater freedom that pupils can use, greater skill as well, as I say to express their feelings, the feelings of others, how they have seen other people feel, either through art or through music. To actually appreciate the sadness in a piece of music means that you can transfer that feeling perhaps to someone's mood when you are talking about how people do change in terms of their mood, how they feel sadness.*

4.0 *CLAIMS ABOUT EFFECTS RELATING TO DEVELOPMENTS IN THE TECHNICAL SKILLS AND CAPABILITIES FOR EACH ARTFORM*

Having outlined three main categories that deal principally with knowledge and understanding, we now turn to three which focus on the purported development of skills. The first of these relates to the acquisition of technical skills for each of the artforms and the arts in general: hence there are six sub-categories.

4.1 Develops technical skills/competence in the arts (unspecified).

Although this sub-category was created to allow for the possibility that interviewees may cite the development of technical skills which were unique to the arts as distinct from individual artforms, in practice, none materialised that could not be assigned to the latter. However, an important point made about most of the artforms is worth making here: many of the teachers interviewed were of the opinion that the development of skills was frequently a necessary precursor to the achievement of other 'second order' outcomes such as heightened self-esteem (see 7.2) and improved competency in expressive skills (see 5.4). The following comment from a deputy head touches on this theme:

> *It should enable children to understand how it is they can express themselves or an idea or a feeling in a different format, in a visual format or in a musical format, and that by learning the skills of painting, of drawing, of reading music, of playing an instrument, of being able to sing or dance, you are developing yourself and developing your ability to express yourself or an idea – whatever – in that format.*

4.2 Develops technical skills/competence in the *VISUAL ARTS*: manipulative skills, motor skills, awareness of form, space, shape, light, tone, texture, colour, skills of observation.

Most teachers of art affirmed that the acquisition of skills was a crucial outcome in their subject and that technical skills were gained and improved upon. Several of the most frequently mentioned examples are presented in the heading of the sub-category.

Selecting the appropriate skills to focus upon as learning outcomes appeared to be related to a set of judgements about such factors as the relevance of skills to different age groups, pupils' previous experiences in art, and differentiation according to ability:

> *In early primary, one of the very, if you like, mechanistic values of painting, drawing and three – dimensional work – it develops motor skills.*

> *I do quite a lot of tonal drawing and they do quite a lot of work in that. I start with that in the first year because I find that junior schools don't appear to have done any of that. That is something that I flog a bit in the first year. It is important.*

> *Less able pupils tend to stay at the first stage of this learning base; more able ones go off on a tangent.*

As indicated above (see 4.1), for several teachers, the teaching and learning of techniques and skills were about offering an empowerment to children, equipping them to achieve other outcomes. Technical skills were seen as enabling pupils by providing them with '*building blocks*':

> *We then provide them with a range of skills in order that they can respond in a visual sense to that sensitivity. Then we give them the opportunity to be able to use those ... facilities to operate in a creative way.*

> *The technical skills [side] is also very important as well, because that gives them the ability to do that* [i.e. be creative].

> *So that colour mixing and being confident about paint – it is about techniques, simple techniques that are magic when you know how to do them ... it was one of those 'Oh, Miss I know how to do this now.' Then each week it is reinforcing what you learnt the last week so you haven't forgotten ... I love the excitement that is generated by something like that happening. They are all going 'That's a really super lesson, Miss. I really learnt.' We sometimes say to them 'Do you think you have learnt anything today?' They say 'I know how to make noses now' or 'How do you make a hand look like it is? Oh, is that what you do?' You know, 'You go home and you do it for homework, you do three of them and then usually you know how to do it.' So it is to do with empowerment, but it is to do with gaining massive amounts of confidence straight away when they say that they can't do it and then they can. So I believe, very much, in showing people really how; I don't leave them to find out for themselves.*

4.3 Develops technical skills/competence in *DANCE*: movement skills, choreographic skills.

Apart from the general skills cited in the heading of this sub-category, the only significant reference to the development of technical skills came from this dance/drama teacher:

> *By the end of key stage 3 ... they know dance terms, they know skills, they know unison, they know where they should use those in a dance, they can create a dance and then what they can do is tell you how they have done it ... it is quite technical when you think about it, to deconstruct work that you have created and say why you have done that when you are 13 years old.*

4.4 Develops technical skills/competence in *DRAMA*: performance skills, improvisation, composition through role play, mime.

Most of the drama teachers volunteered the acquisition of skills as an outcome of their teaching. Although there was a noticeable reticence about using the term 'theatrical skills', by far the most common reference to outcomes associated with skills was 'performance skills'. Examples included:

One is the performance skills, because when it comes down to it, [drama and dance] *are performance subjects and to give, not just pupils but anyone, the skills in which to perform confidently* [is important] ... *I feel that they need to have those skills to make sure that the product is worth presenting. I think that that then feeds back and makes my job easier, in fact, because if pupils are performing in different areas and other people are watching when they come to the lessons, then there is an expectation and there is a level of commitment and a standard that they then aim at. I don't have to keep reinforcing it; it is already there.*

I also over the years have realised the enormous responsibility you have, as soon as you put your pupils on the stage. You're not doing them a favour if they're not performing well, and that's important to teach them those skills.

In the end, what the kids can achieve is very, very meaningful performance.

One teacher volunteered that *'we do teach theatre skills'*, but qualified it by adding that this was only to a limited extent and that they were not taught in isolation, but as part of topics on substantive themes. Another teacher also pointed to both theatrical skills and dramatic techniques as important outcomes: *'how we put the words on the stage, how we structure things, the different techniques that we use to get that across'*. Another identified the ability to write a play: *'Well there are the technical skills that if they wanted to make a play at any point in the rest of their lives they could do so.'*

4.5 Develops technical skills/competence in *ENGLISH.*
There was only one reference to any claimed effects on technical skills that were perceived to have any relevance to the processes of creative composition in English:

[When discussing skills in grammar and punctuation] *I think those secretarial skills are very, very central to creativity, because they help to clarify and language is not just a mish-mash of half-expressed utterances – if you haven't got the correct word and you haven't got the right punctuation, really you can't express and very often the finest, say, with a Larkin poem within the complexity of the syntax and so on is something that allows the poem to hang together ... the school inspection brought this up; she said that we are very good on the secretarial things* (head of English).

Interestingly, apart from this comment, there were no references to technical skills associated with the actual processes involved in the making and invention of text, compared, for example, with those identified for art.

4.6   Develops technical skills/competence in *MUSIC*: learning to play musical instruments, notation, keyboard skills, pitch, rhythm, compositional skills, performance skills.

Perhaps even more than art, music was awash with alleged outcomes in technical skills. Those listed in the heading were often mentioned; others included: learning to read music, musical form, percussion, coordination and dexterity and auditory skills.

As was evident in the art teachers' responses, many music teachers also seemed to adhere to the principle of building up the technical skills gradually and progressively to facilitate the achievement of other 'second-order' effects, such as self-expression and creativity:

> *So what I do is to try to expose them to, like, simple things, like the concepts of pitch and rhythm – things like that. So eventually, I am leading them to self-expression, but not in the first term of Year 7.*

There were, however, suggestions that not all teachers of music were comfortable with a view of curriculum progression which meant that creativity and self-expression were postponed until minimum standards of technical skills had been achieved. An alternative approach to the sequencing of learning outcomes was offered by one interviewee:

> *Pupils pick up the technical skills through the activity in many respects. I tend to teach technique and knowledge, if you like, on a very much on a need to know basis* (deputy head).

5.0   *CLAIMS ABOUT EFFECTS RELATING TO DEVELOPMENTS IN COMMUNICATION AND EXPRESSIVE SKILLS*

The four sub-categories in this type of outcome cover the arts in general and all of the individual artforms.

5.1   Develops (interactive) communication skills.

Although there were some references to this effect from across the artforms, drama attracted far more than any other area. It was claimed that in drama pupils learn to convey a wide range of content messages through a variety of forms of communication (e.g. verbal and non-verbal signals). One drama teacher expressed it as follows:

> *When they have suddenly found they can communicate ideas, meanings, atmosphere, subtext, emotion, through just themselves as like an instrument, I suppose our body is our instrument, as they say.*

The development of such skills was seen as highly relevant to the current and future needs of young people:

> *I see drama as a means of people engaging with the world around them ... and in that way hopefully develop them to analyse and communicate interactively*

with what is around them, and to question, and to sometimes enjoy praise. To do that you have to give the tools of drama, because the power in the drama comes when people actually feel it as well as think it and then they say 'Oh gosh, yes'... it has become more important as the world around the kids has become more complex; their ability to engage in, receive, question and communicate in an intelligible way is becoming more and more important (head of drama).

A deputy head in one school emphasised that drama is an important means of improving the communication skills of pupils for whom English is not their first language:

> *I think that the importance ... for a child for whom English is not a first language, with a philosophy that our drama people have about performance and drama, and commitment, and cooperation, and working together. In terms of building confidence, so the child who cannot attack the writing on the page can communicate, can be part of, can begin to grow and develop in confidence as part of the teamwork and collaboration of drama, [it] has a huge impact on that child's experience on expectation and what happens.*

To support the case for the claim that drama develops communication skills, one interviewee relayed evidence given by a group of drama GCSE pupils who were involved in a course run for major employers and industrialists in the area:

> *Afterwards the industrialists then asked the kids why did they choose to do drama and the kids were talking about teamwork ... bless them, sometimes you could just kiss them. Clearly we could not prime them; they were not primed and these kids talked about the ability to communicate, to be confident and all that* (LEA adviser).

5.2   Encourages development of language, speech, eloquence.

This sub-category represents an extension to the previous one in that it concentrates more specifically on outcomes relating to language and speech rather than the more general and interactive communication skills. Again, it was dominated by the perceived effects of drama. There were several references to speech, speaking with clarity, eloquence and (less frequently) elocution:

> *Speech skills: we did a lot of direct speech on 'fair is foul and foul is fair'; you've actually got to get your tongue round that so we can actually do a bit of elocution – almost and they enjoy doing it* (drama teacher).

Not all drama teachers, however, would want to promote the elocution aspect of speech development as an appropriate outcome for their subject:

> *If they say to me it is about elocution, or it is about putting on plays, or it is about facing the front, my answers are definitely no. You know, it is just not, it is never that; it is about helping kids develop and making sense of the world around them and engaging with it. That is that; they have got to have some tools to work with that makes it work. Otherwise it is just me and it is not*

theirs; they can't own it if they haven't made it ... it is a bit of a sort of coming together rather than clarity and there are certain things that I know that it definitely cannot be, like elocution (laughter).

In one school, accounts from the headteacher and the drama teacher corroborated the perception that drama was having a significant impact on the capacity of the pupils to articulate their opinions and to speak confidently in public:

> *I think that the pupils here are very assertive, very confident, and I think that a lot of that has to do with the work that they do in drama. We get loads of visitors into the school and the pupils here will talk to anybody. At the public meeting that we had here last night, one of our little Year 7s put up her hand and said 'I want to say something' and made a really pertinent contribution. The director of education said I think that is probably the best contribution that we have had so far tonight; it was just superb. There is a real level of confidence here from the pupils* (headteacher).

> *I think that pupils are articulating themselves. I think this is one of the strengths of our school, that they articulate themselves very well. I think there is a gap between how they write and how they actually express themselves. I think that drama has contributed to that because we have put things on in a public situation, in like assemblies, in year meetings. They are taking drama outside of the school and I think then that other pupils see that and that feeds back into it* (drama teacher).

More generally, interviewees from across the artforms cited the development of languages and vocabularies to assist pupils in their discourses about works of art and the processes of creating them. Such references had much in common with the growth in knowledge, understanding and appreciation of the arts which were recorded under Category 1. The following was one such comment:

> *This is the second year that drama and dance have been together, and what I am noticing is that the language that pupils are using has expanded and they are crossing over. So when they are dancing, they are talking about audience; they are talking about creating atmosphere. In drama, they are talking about body shapes and travelling, so the two are crossing over* (dance and drama teacher).

5.3   Develops critical/active listening and interpretative skills, listens to others.
Drama was also at the forefront of claims about the growth in the skills of listening to others. This headteacher saw this outcome as having a moderating effect on some young people:

> *... one of the things that I find quite interesting is how youngsters will sometimes moderate ...* [they are] *very confident to start with in drama,* [but] *will probably develop the skills of listening to others more and reflection.*

5.4 Develops expressive skills, helps learners make statements (about the/their world, themselves), self-expression, confidence to express.

With numerous references from across the different artforms, this perceived effect was one of the most frequently nominated of all the sub-categories. Essentially, it focused on the empowerment young people were deemed to gain through being encouraged to express themselves, their opinions, their ideas, their values and their creativity. Interviewees saw the arts as occupying a crucial place in the curriculum largely because they offered children the space and the 'freedom' to express their perspectives on themselves and their world. One headteacher captured the views of many when talking about the power of the arts to enable the making and articulating of personal statements:

> *Many of the curriculum subjects are to do with children responding to, and reacting to, a world upon which they have little influence and have little that they can record in a personal, subjective way. The strength of the arts is it is something that they take in; it is their response to the world which they must digest and put out again.*

Arts-oriented outlets and media for self-expression were especially important for groups of pupils who, for various reasons, would otherwise find the making and communicating of personal statements difficult. One example centred on the opportunity given to pupils with limited academic ability or children for whom English is not a first language to 'open up' in arts subjects that do not require writing. Other examples included:

> *My aims are to work with the young people in a way that they don't usually get to work with others, which enables them then to find a different way of expressing themselves. We are always finding that there are people who cannot express themselves in other areas and maybe they are put down because of that, but they can really flourish in drama* (head of drama).

> *For example in the performing arts, I think you can take a child who might, for example, I can think of examples where pupils are maybe – have a small circle of friends, have maybe a slightly eccentric personality, maybe a little bit precocious even, or maybe a little bit more mature than their years would suggest they should be, finding an opportunity maybe in acting or theatre work which allows them to express all those things which are not possible perhaps with their peers* (head of Welsh).

> [Talking about the visual arts] *They can express themselves in ways that does not mean that they have to stand up on a stage and perform, nor are they going to have to sort of expose themselves to other individuals, as it were, in the way that they do in drama* (ex head of art).

> *You know kids are so often not allowed to express how they feel, you know, if they are angry they are not allowed to go and thump someone because you just don't do that, that isn't right. They are not allowed to express by crying, because it is just not cool to cry. The arts, you know, dance, they can express*

how they feel in it; maybe it's one way that they can actually let go of some of their emotions (dance and PE teacher).

Sometimes it does seem that the kids who are the bad kids in other subjects, because they are the disruptive ones, are the ones who do really well in our subjects because that expression, that freedom of expression, is what they relish and they are away (drama teacher).

A recurring theme through the comments recorded under this sub-category was a perception, for some a strong conviction, that the development of expression through the arts was extremely enabling for young people (e.g. through offering an alternative language, a '*voice or voices*', an internal locus of control or a release of personal tensions and inhibitions). The following are just a selection of many such observations:

[It is about] *finding a means of expressing themselves, and looking at the world around them, and coming to terms with that. You are equipping them with sophisticated tools and, as I said, for me personally* [theatre] *is not the be all and end all; it is not about them being able to act particularly well or whatever. It is being able to manipulate those tools for their own means, so being able to do that, they feel that they have more control over what they are doing* (head of drama).

They've got an outlet for expressing themselves which makes them more relaxed about life, in control of life (drama teacher).

[Music gives] *a way of expressing what you have inside, if that makes sense. It is like ... not feelings, it is just a way ... it is another language. It is another language and I have just gained so much enjoyment from it, just being able to play and sing. I think that it is a way of release as well, I think that every child should have the opportunity to experience that* (head of music).

There also seemed to be general agreement about the value and, for some, the necessity, of building the capacity for self-expression on the firm foundations of the acquisition of the technical skills outlined in Category 4. For some interviewees, these were construed as the essential 'tools' of expression and a key outcome of arts education was seen as enabling pupils to decide which set of tools best suited each individual's endeavours to be expressive:

Here I am, up in the Lake District, and I'm moved by the sunrise, over by Lake Conniston, and unless I have got the ability ... and I may not have experienced poetry, but I might be quite an accomplished musician, I cannot write a poem about that because I simply don't have the tools. I cannot work in that way, because nobody has given me the tools to respond like that. So all I have got to do is to write it in music and to express my response in music. That may not be appropriate. Why is it that Wordsworth reacted in the way that he did to his surroundings? Is it because he didn't have a decent music education? We will never know that ... so unless we can give kids a chance to know how they can respond, and think, and work out, or what their preferred mode of activity is, then those ideas may forever just stay locked inside them; there is no way of actually exploring that (LEA adviser).

From the dramatic point of view, they have acquired the confidence and the skill to be able to know what is a good way of, either in role play or themselves, being able to express themselves (deputy head).

The different [art] forms in which you can express these ideas or explore these ideas within the classroom and the analysis of that, and how a child coming into a secondary school has very, very limited knowledge of that artform, if any, and through the five years, or even through the three years if they don't opt to do it for GCSE, they then have the tools in which to express a variety of ideas, well endless ideas really, in a form (drama teacher).

In several respects, however, there was a lack of consensus in the implicit messages conveyed about the precise nature of this claimed effect. While some seemed to suggest that the effect was the 'opportunity' for self-expression, others appeared to believe that the outcome was a set of positive attitudes and predispositions in young people to be expressive. Still others implied that self-expression was the application of technical skills to the making of personal statements, whereas some seemed to insinuate that there may be a set of competencies labelled 'expressive skills' that exist over and above the artform technical skills. These various interpretations of expressive outcomes carry important implications for any attempts to substantiate these claimed effects.

6.0 *CLAIMS ABOUT EFFECTS RELATING TO DEVELOPMENTS IN THE CAPACITIES FOR THINKING, PROBLEM-SOLVING AND CREATIVITY*

This category encompasses claims about the impact of the arts on high-order cognitive skills and competencies. It contains two sub-categories.

6.1 Develops thinking, abstract thinking, logical argument, thought processes, reflection, internalising, making sense of/responding to/representing the world mentally, interpretation processes, cognitive ability, problem-solving skills.

This alleged outcome also attracted numerous citations. It was widely held that the arts encourage children to grow intellectually, to think critically by fostering the challenging of ideas and perceptions, to interpret and analyse in depth, to think '*off the top of their heads*' and to think laterally and divergently (which links with 6.2 on creativity). For many, the arts were seen as developing the ability to ask questions such as '*Why should it be like that?*' and '*Why are we doing this?*' They also develop the ability to look at problems and around problems – in the words of one interviewee, '*the ability to think expansively*'. A number of interviewees stressed the role of the arts in facilitating a subjective internalisation process through which pupils can be helped to construct their meanings of the world:

It is subjective, because it is an internalising process, and the arts cannot get away from that. It is that interpretation of the world; that is its fundamental thing – in a way that other areas of the curriculum cannot be used to help children interpret and internalise (head).

You are giving them the scope to look at it from a different way, and to really give a much deeper understanding of what is happening because they are internalising more, delving deeper into the concepts beneath what is happening (head of drama).

I think it is in this developing youngsters' self-confidence and tolerance, the ability of youngsters to reflect and think. Also be prepared to let youngsters understand, I think, that they have internalised our ethos; and internalising things is one of the features of arts education, isn't it? (head).

As touched on in this last extract, some interviewees, including some headteachers, noted the development of reflection as an important outcome.

It slows things down; it slows things down in a way that allows one to stand and take stock of what one is doing. That is a very important skill. In a lot of the technological related subjects, we are at the next stage and it is hitting us before we know it, because the technology is there that takes us that way. Reflection.

Some teachers saw problem-solving as an intended aim and effect associated with most of the artforms:

Problem solving, be it a piece of art work, be it trying to make a piece of music from some ideas, or the drama, this is the theme we are working on; it is problem solving, in space and shape and dance (deputy head).

I think that the main thing that I am hoping to achieve is some sort of independence and autonomy, so that they possess their work, they have got some sort of feeling that it is their ownership. They are generating something for themselves that they want to do and through that they are exploring all sorts of creative, imaginative sides and bringing in all sorts of problem solving skills, that sort of thing (art teacher).

6.2 Develops creativity, imagination, confidence to create, taking risks, unknown outcomes, freedom of experimentation, can make mistakes.

This sub-category amounted to a major claimed effect. In one way or another, nearly all the interviewees concurred that one of the main intended outcomes of arts education was to give pupils '*the confidence to create*' and the '*ability to create*'. Learning to experiment in the spirit of exploration and take risky steps into the unknown was held to be at the heart of achieving this outcome:

... they learn to risk take and not be devastated if the results are not so great; they get a huge buzz when it is great (deputy head).

Art is a bit like science: there is an experimental side and there is an applied side. Graphics is very much the applied aspects of the experimental work that goes within the fine art areas. Without the experimentation, without the involvement of investigation into work of other artists, knowledge of critical and contextual implications of what is going on, then what you do becomes very sterile in an applied sense (ex head of art).

It's just asking questions – how are you going to translate something you see in front of you or whatever, an idea, a feeling, down on to a piece of paper, a canvas, material, whatever? That translation process and just working it through it and just seeing all the different ways and just exploring – and having the confidence to do different – try different things, make mistakes and experiment and get to a final conclusion (head of art).

The mental processes which accompany the realisation that there are important areas of human endeavour which are not susceptible to uniform 'right or wrong' answers were another important outcome for many:

Well I think it can develop children, pupils, to give them a sense of their surroundings, a sense of self-confidence as well, which I think is very important. I always try and get across there's no right or wrongs, there's always questions and you've got to answer them in your own way, so it's quite a venture of self-discovery sometimes doing a piece of art work and we can all draw the same objects in the centre of the room, but come out with a totally different piece of work – and that's fine (head of art).

In a similar vein, several teachers referred to the fostering of the related capacity for making 'imaginative' responses:

We like to create an atmosphere where they can be creative and use their imagination (ex head of art).

It is something that is inside their head; it's an imaginative life, a creative life that [drama] *gives them* (drama teacher).

Some added, however, that developing creativity and the capacity to initiate the processes of exploration required the acquisition of technical skills (see Category 4) and an understanding of artforms and their contexts (see Category 1). One teacher attempted to explore the relationship between creative faculties, technical skills and a critical appreciation of the artform:

It is learning to think in lots of different ways. Creative thinking I would say is one of the things that they do get from us and all the usual investigating ... I don't really know how I can explain creative thinking, except that it is something that grows as you point out ways of looking, doing, making. The next time they know it or they are more creative in their own ... they don't just think of one way ... we always try and develop ideas in more than one way at the same time. So, if they are doing that big portrait, for instance, that I just said, then they would be trying out the same idea in their sketch book several ways before they make a final decision ... if you are there day in and day out doing this and you can see something happening, but it is very hard for me to tell you what is happening, but I could see at the end of two years the difference. It is very often reminding people about what we have done before and how we thought then, or what you thought about this, or did you see and take in that? ... it is to do with building up in your little computer in your head, I suppose, a whole load of information?... (head of expressive arts).

7.0 *CLAIMS ABOUT EFFECTS RELATING TO PERSONAL DEVELOPMENT AND SELF-AWARENESS*

Having considered three categories that focused on knowledge and understanding (Categories 1-3) and three that dealt with different types of skills (Categories 4-6), we now turn to outline two that relate to the growth in self-awareness (Category 7) and personal skills (Category 8).

7.1 Develops an understanding of one's self, one's uniqueness, promotes individuality.

This was another prevalent claim among teachers of most of the artforms. Finding out or discovering about your 'self' as a result of arts education was a common theme: phrases like '*greater awareness of themselves*', '*feeling comfortable with themselves*' were used quite regularly. Other contributions included:

[With reference to drama] *Very often, for a lot of them, they have just found out a little bit more about themselves. And they've begun to discover themselves in a way that maybe they are never given the opportunity to do* (drama teacher).

[Again with reference to drama] *The most important thing I think is that they come out and they feel they know more about themselves and about what is going on around them and they can respond to that* (head of drama).

The pupils also are allowed to develop individually. One of the sixth-formers, for example, I know has been doing things – sculpting out of wood, tree trunks and this sort of thing – which one doesn't find very often, but which is very appropriate for this area – totem poles and this type of thing are being looked at (deputy head).

It allows for individualistic ideas and views, it helps to create self-images which are important for people (head).

[With reference to the visual arts] *It's that gain in confidence in themselves, knowing themselves a bit more – I can't explain it, but I can see them develop and coming out of themselves, because it's a horrible age I think, growing up, being a teenager and being confident enough to be an individual and to do things. I really do think it does help* (head of art).

One adviser extended this type of impact beyond the general effect of 'knowing your self' to the more specific outcome of 'knowing what you know', 'knowing your own intuition' and 'knowing your own values' through the channel of metacognition:

> *Critically, the notion of metacognition, of knowing what you know, being aware of what you're aware of, because so often our intuition is down there somewhere, we are not always in touch with it, so I think if they can be in touch with their own intuition, their own selves.*

One headteacher offered a potent image of how the arts make a distinctive contribution to the development of a student's individuality:

> *When it is an art process, they have made those changes themselves, it is part of them that has made it and that ... and their signature is all over the piece of work in a way that it isn't over a piece of science or maths. That is an important bit, the signature bit ... this is something that only you can produce because you are you, and you are unique. Maybe that is it, the uniqueness of the individual; maybe that is why in certain societies, art is always distrusted as a dangerous thing.*

7.2 Fosters a sense of self-worth, self-esteem, pride, valuing of one's self, validation of the child/learner, sense of achievement – higher than expected achievements (in the arts) can be reached, transcends reliance on literacy and numeracy.

This significant and frequent claim was made by teachers from across all artforms, and relates to a number of other perceived aims or outcomes, particularly enjoyment (11.1), and the development of expressive skills (5.4).

Numerous references were made to the capacity of the arts to foster positive self-images in pupils. Some responses referred generally to 'self-esteem', but interestingly, the majority of claims for this effect coupled the enhancement of self-esteem with achievement (be it personal achievements such as painting a picture or performing, or recognised qualifications such as GCSEs). Often, the implication was that all children can achieve in the arts in some way, particularly those who are low achievers in subjects other than the arts:

> *... poor ability children ... can't quite believe what they have produced in art. They are really impressed by what they have done, because they don't achieve an awful lot in other subjects* (art teacher).

> *... a boy in Year 11 who has a stutter and has really done nothing until the final exam piece, when he got really involved, and his self-esteem has just gone through the roof. He is just a changed man really ... and things like that are exciting as well* (head of drama).

> *... there are so many opportunities within the arts for pupils to achieve, whether it is qualifications, certificates, in extra-curricular activities, as well*

as the obvious things, such as GCSEs. Also achievement is standing up there, I feel, in front of an audience of people and doing your best (deputy head).

As this last quote indicates, performance was identified as an aspect of the arts which can foster a sense of self-worth or develop self-esteem:

> *... drama but also performance as well. I think performance enhances your self-esteem quite often – if you at the age of 14 and 15 can stand in front of a full hall and give a credible performance, whatever the length, I think that's a feather in anybody's cap. It is for an adult and I think, given that experience of finding a way of feeling good about yourself or feeling that you've shown that you're able to do something and do it well, it's always good, it's a positively reinforcing experience* (head of Welsh).

One teacher saw the enhancement of self-esteem as a result of the philosophy behind teaching in the arts, where everybody is valued:

> *... because of the philosophy about how they are taught, and what you bring is valued, what you are is valued and that those are positive, very positive starting points. So I think in terms of achievement, confidence and expectation it all moves forward* (deputy head).

Another, a music teacher, rather epigrammatically, stated: '*Creativity is a sense of achievement*', whilst other teachers implied – perhaps rather idealistically – that pupils do not compare their achievements unfavourably with those of others in the arts, or feel frustrated by their lack of ability. This music teacher made a distinction between other subjects and music:

> *They can all start from a very equal place. I don't see that the same in other subjects, perhaps it is, but when you know you are doing simpler maths than the next person, you somehow know that you are not quite achieving the same; you know that you are eventually going to have to do their question next, but they will be on to the next question. You put a group together in music. Now they know that certain people – okay, we have got some people who have had piano lessons, and they are working in a group, but they know that their part is absolutely 100 per cent vital. They may only be playing the bass drum, but without them the keyboard means nothing. You may be playing a fabulous part, but without me you are nobody. I think that the fact that you can use arts like that, you know that there is satisfaction and you can get through to anybody who wants to try in the subject.*

7.3 Fosters a sense of self-confidence:
(a) in an unspecified way

Closely related to the fostering and development of self-esteem, this sub-category focuses more specifically on claims for the arts in developing self-confidence. This 'unspecified' sub-category contained the many references to the arts '*building confidence*', where the nature of the increased confidence was not elaborated on, for example:

> *Yes, I think that in this particular school, building self confidence with quite a lot of the girls, especially maybe the Bengali girls, who are very quiet on the whole – I think for us to give them that kind of confidence is the main thing maybe that they get out of it* (head of expressive arts).

In some cases, teachers illustrated this effect of the arts on particular pupils, with one teacher describing the letters received from parents after drama courses which told of their children's growth in confidence.

There was a particular emphasis in this category on drama. For instance, one drama teacher was aware of the often-cited effect of 'drama builds confidence', and appeared keen to extend this further:

> *Well, I would place some emphasis on confidence, even though I don't mean it in quite the same glib way as I often see it kind of jotted down – 'Drama gives you confidence' – but I think it's a kind of inner thing, inner confidence, which is that 'I can say what I think as long as I say it sensibly and I really mean what I say'. It's not necessarily about speaking loudly and being heard, but about 'Actually I know that my ideas are interesting and, however I share those ideas, I'm going to be appreciated and understood'; so it's a sort of confidence: I'd really like to call it a quiet confidence. But sometimes it also manifests itself in a big confidence which is 'I'll volunteer for things'.*

Again, the 'building confidence' aspect of the arts was perceived by some to be particularly important for pupils with English as a second language, and for those with lower attainment in non-arts subjects.

(b) in their own abilities

This sub-category is closely related to 7.2, since a 'sense of achievement', 'self-esteem' and 'confidence in one's own abilities' are clearly linked.

One teacher valued assessment as an avenue through which pupils can realise their achievements and abilities, which were often considered to be of a higher level than they initially thought they were capable of. Teachers also linked this confidence with the acquisition of technical skills in the artform:

> *We sometimes say to them 'Do you think you have learnt anything today?' ... it is to do with empowerment, but it is to do with gaining massive amounts of confidence straightaway when they say that they can't do it and then they can. So I believe, very much, in showing people really how; I don't leave them to find out for themselves* (head of expressive arts).

(c) in their capacity to perform (in front of others)

Specific mentions of confidence with regard to performance were made by some teachers, particularly by teachers of music, drama and dance. One teacher stated an aim as: '*... to give, not just pupils but anyone, the skills in which to perform confidently*' (dance and drama teacher).

7.4   Develops whole personality, balanced person, decision-making/quality of life based on breadth of experience and opportunities, character building.

The last sub-category concerned with self-awareness covered claims made that the arts *'... develop[s] them so much as people'* (music teacher). Responses were frequent across the artforms, but were often general rather than specific, for example:

> *... learning about becoming an adult ...* (deputy head).

> *I think the personality with the imagination needed for arts; I think a personality is enriched beyond anything if they have art, music or drama ...* (head of music).

> *It's very difficult to break it down but I think it's developing the whole person and enabling them when they leave school here to become more responsible and to put them, shall we say, ready for life after school* (deputy head).

> *I think that the arts are really quite important there in terms of spiritual development and just having examples of the arts ... in terms of developing whole pupils, I think that it really is very important. It is more than just the academic results that I think arts contributes to* (headteacher).

More specific responses identified 'issues' as an aspect of arts education contributing to pupils' personal development, and also to the creative writing process:

> *an artform which embraces all the birth, life and death issues that we all live ... [it] enables us to engage with those things, to reflect upon them and to see ourselves in relation to those things* (LEA arts adviser).

> *Well I would hope that it would help their own mental and spiritual economy in the sense that creative writing should help the individual's psychology and growth and development* (head of English).

The intangible nature of this effect was acknowledged by some teachers, for example: *'... I don't know – it is hard to put it into words really, what it is that is happening while they are there'* (head of expressive arts).

A second aspect of this sub-category links to Category 2.1, broadening horizons and perspectives. Again there was recognition of the part the arts can play in *'... people doing things that they wouldn't have the chance to do'* (deputy head). This same interviewee went on to say:

> *... there are kids here whose eyes, in spite of what I said before about them coming generally from more aware homes now, kids whose eyes and experiences are opened by the opportunities that they have been given here, even the fairly limited ones that we are able to give them.*

And, referring to work done with a sculptor:

The notion of having statues on the lawn outside was 'What is this doing at [school]?' You know this is what they do in Oxford, or somewhere like that ... the kids were quite proud to have their statues there, that people noticed when they came here. Now that is just one small example of how you can lift awareness and change an outlook.

8.0 *CLAIMS ABOUT EFFECTS RELATING TO PERSONAL QUALITIES AND SKILLS*

This category was developed to account for effects relating to personal qualities and skills, as opposed to technical skills, and communication or social skills. However, few interviewees made claims specifically for growth in personal qualities through arts education.

8.1 Develops a sense of responsibility, taking initiative.

Two interviewees in management cited the development of responsibility as an effect of arts education.

8.2 Enhances organisational skills.

There were also two responses where teachers claimed that the arts enhance organisational skills.

8.3 Develops independence and autonomy, ownership.

This third sub-category was made up of the more frequently claimed effect relating to ownership. The arts were seen to provide opportunities for pupils to have ownership of their experiences in ways in which they may not in other curriculum areas. Some teachers related this to independence and autonomy:

... the main thing that I am hoping to achieve is some sort of independence and autonomy, so that they possess their work, they have got some sort of feeling that it is their ownership (visual art teacher).

9.0 *CLAIMS ABOUT EFFECTS RELATING TO INCREASES IN THE AWARENESS OF OTHER PEOPLE*

Moving on from claims that the arts develop self-awareness and personal skills, Categories 9 and 10 include claimed effects about relating to others: awareness of other people (Category 9), and the development of social skills (Category 10).

9.1 Encourages tolerance.

Although this sub-category was developed to account for responses which saw tolerance as an effect distinguishable from other effects related to awareness of others, in closer analysis of the data, only one response addressed tolerance specifically. This was with reference to tolerance and respect of other cultures and of the art work of others.

9.2 Develops sensitivity.

As above, this sub-category was also only appropriate for one response.

9.3 Develops empathy, seeing things from another perspective, broadening 'out-of-self' horizons, valuing of others, valuing others' work.

In contrast to the sparseness of responses in the above sub-categories, a number of interviewces made claims about the arts developing empathy and the ability to see things from other perspectives.

Two distinct types of responses emerged: those which focused on appreciating and valuing the work of others, for example '*I try to put across to them the importance of not destroying another person's work*', and those which concentrated on the aspect of seeing things from another perspective, for example '*I think they begin to learn that kind of consideration for the points of view of others*'; '*... to understand the other's predicament*'. Differences between the artforms were evident here, and thus this sub-category is explored further in the subsequent chapter looking at variation by artform.

10.0 *CLAIMS ABOUT EFFECTS RELATING TO THE DEVELOPMENT OF SOCIAL SKILLS*

Two large sub-categories occurred within this category, dealing with claimed effects for the arts relating to group work and improved social skills and relationships. There were links with Category 5 (developments in communication and expressive skills).

10.1 Improves the capacity to work as a group, teamwork, intra-group trust, reliability, realises power of groups.

Teachers across the artforms commented on the opportunities that the arts provide for pupils to work in groups and develop group identity through playing in school bands, working on productions and undertaking shared experiences in lesson time:

> *And they work in groups: they've got to communicate with one another and work it out, which is quite nice for them to work in groups, rather then in isolation all the time. They have to discuss ideas and things* (art teacher).

> *... the drama side where people work together to create a performance or to work together on a feeling or a situation and then express it* (head of Welsh).

One music teacher claimed that they produce a lot of people who work well together as musicians, which is not always the same as being a great player. Another teacher told of how experiences in drama had helped to unite a form group:

> *One kid in a Year 9 group, who are appalling at listening, cannot listen to save their lives – we have a battle every week. But they're great. When they get going they are a good group, and she said to me 'It's brought the form together'... it brings them together as a unit, it brings them together understanding each other working together.*

41

An interesting aim was put forward by one teacher: to get pupils to work together and *'pull together'* but paralleling this, to have departments do the same, so that pupils do not see any separation between arts subjects. This echoes the points raised in 1.6 about links and integration within the arts.

Another aspect of this sub-category was the development of the skills of group work such as cooperation, negotiation within a group, getting on with people, leadership skills and listening (see Category 5). One teacher expressed the view that mixed-ability arts lessons provide good opportunities for all, and another described pupils *'sparking'* off each other.

10.2   Develops social skills, relationships, making friends.

As well as providing opportunities for working together, and the development of 'group work skills', claims were made by some teachers for the arts enhancing social skills and personal relationships. For some, this was on the very practical level of giving pupils a wider circle of friends; for others, including this headteacher, it was a more abstract concept:

> *I think the art education in some ways allows ... people to get closer as people ... it is more than individualistic, an understanding of each other's natures, calming, and understanding more of the nature of people.*

In drama, there was a focus on understanding relationships through role plays and characterisation:

> *I am hoping it will keep them out of trouble, but will also benefit them to play each situation for what it is so when they are in the interview situation or they're, you know, at a party or whatever, they can play that situation and feel comfortable with themselves and perhaps hopefully understand other people around them* (drama teacher).

One drama teacher described the learning taking place as a *'life skill'*:

> *I mean it's going back to the people thing again, isn't it? You can't actually do drama on your own, and you learn that through the five years that it's the fusion between my idea and your idea that makes something good, and that's probably a life skill isn't it.*

10.3   Challenges taboos (e.g. boys touching, physical contact).
This small category accounted for responses from dance and drama teachers, where they addressed the issue of the gender imbalance in dance and drama participation, and actively encouraged boys' involvement.

10.4   Sees staff as real people, breaks barriers down between teacher and student, improves communication between teachers and pupils.
An effect of the arts mentioned particularly by music teachers was the relationship that can develop between teacher and student. One head of department described shared music making as '*magical chemistry*'.

11.0   *CLAIMS ABOUT EFFECTS RELATING TO IMPROVEMENTS IN GENERAL WELL-BEING*
Intrinsic effects of the arts such as improvements in well-being are covered in this category, which is made up of three sub-categories: the enjoyment factor, therapeutic outcomes, and enhanced physical fitness. The first of these attracted a particularly high number of nominations.

11.1   Makes people happier, gives enjoyment, fulfilment, fun, more to life than work/shopping/materialism, pleasure.
Numerous responses across the arts focused on '*enjoyment*', '*fun*' and the adrenaline rush or '*buzz*' that can come from involvement in the arts.

This category links to 7.2, in the sense that teachers suggested that it was often the fact that pupils could be more successful in the arts than they were in other subjects that precipitated the experience of enjoyment, that is, a sense of achievement is part of the enjoyment factor. Enjoyment was also identified as the common element for children of different abilities in the arts:

> *A child who is Grade 8 Distinction violin in Year 8, he's going to get so many more different things out of the classroom lesson than somebody who may be level 5 statement, but at the end of the day they should be both enjoying it* (head of music).

There was also a recognition by teachers of their own enjoyment and love for the arts that manifests itself in their teaching. One music teacher used the pronoun 'we' when describing the enjoyment that comes from creating music: '*We have a wonderful time; it is ever such fun making ... creating this music ...*'

One head of music cited enjoyment as an important part of the school's inclusive attitude to the arts: '*... as I said, it's an arts for all policy; it's just basically "Get involved and enjoy it" and get out what you can get out of it.*'

There was also recognition from some teachers of the dimension added to pupils' lives through their involvement in the arts:

... another dimension to their lives, which isn't just a factual, mechanical dimension. It is something that is a life inside their head; it's an imaginative life, a creative life that it gives them (drama teacher).

So that at the end of a production, they are crying, a 17-year-old lad is crying, because something he knows is wonderful in his life, a major part in a school production, has ended on the Saturday night. Now, that sort of effect on someone has got to be life-changing and that is an outcome that I would want (headteacher).

11.2   Offers therapeutic outcomes, releases tension, de-stresses, deep calm, relaxing escapism.

Interestingly, responses that fitted this sub-category came predominantly from one school, and from one teacher in particular. This head of expressive arts saw the arts as having therapeutic value, and a calming effect, enabling student to go into their '*own little world*'. From the same school, a deputy head perceived the arts as offering pupils an escape, albeit a temporary one, from the trials of everyday life:

You know, poor housing, unemployment – all those things that these young people's families cope with – and the kids tend to leave that at the gate and come in and get on with learning. And it does offer, in the same sense, that all of those arts subjects are in a sense are escaping from this into whatever piece of work you are doing. It offers an opportunity to put those things behind for a while and look at things again (deputy head).

11.3   Enhances physical health, fitness, strength, endurance, body awareness, physical confidence.

This category was developed to account for the handful of responses from dance teachers which talked about the effect that dance has on developing movement, coordination, endurance and strength. One described this as developing knowledge about '*how to treat bodies*'.

12.0   *CLAIMS RELATING TO EXTRAPOLATION OR TRANSFER EFFECTS*

This last category in the typology of claimed effects on pupils covers a range of 'transfer effects'.

12.1   Improves performance in other areas of the curriculum/academic areas through unspecified ways.

This sub-category was developed to account for general and unspecific claims that the arts improve performance, for example:

... how it is good in its own right, but how it does benefit everything else (deputy headteacher).

The teaching and the learning styles that are used within arts will rub off in other areas (deputy headteacher).

12.2 Improves performance in other areas of the curriculum/academic areas through increased general motivation to school/work, increased self-discipline, better attitudes, behaviour.

Claims were made for the arts generally helping to engender positive attitudes to school and the classroom environment. A deputy headteacher commented that by taking an interest in pupils' arts involvement, '*... they tend to react and become more pro school*'. A headteacher spoke of the arts helping a student with a '*school phobia problem*':

> *I've got him back into school now three days a week – not into classes, just got him into the school. Now, next two weeks he's got a target of coming to school five days a week, but he's going to be an assistant tutor with the artists and the primary school children – art is motivating him.*

Teachers commented on arts involvement having an effect on self-confidence, and raising aspirations in other areas.

12.3 Improves performance in other areas of the curriculum/academic areas through transference of skills and knowledge (e.g. presentation of written work, research skills, stage lighting technological skills).

This sub-category amounted to a major claimed effect, with some teachers describing the transference of skills and knowledge as '*knock-on effects*'. This sub-category links with the categories that discuss the original direct effect, for example, technical skills (Category 4), thinking skills (6.1) and group work (10.1).

Claims made for the transfer of skills from the arts to other curriculum areas tended to be artform-specific, and interesting differences by artform in both frequency of claims about transfer effects, and in the types of transfer claimed, are explored in Chapter 3. Interestingly, although one head of music indicated that s/he had seen research where it had been '*proven*' that listening to music and learning an instrument increases ability in all subjects, there were minimal references by teachers to research in the area of transfer effects. It would thus appear that teachers hold genuine views about the capacity for the arts to transfer to other curriculum areas, and that it is not the recent attention given to such research in the media that led to this category being a major claimed effect. However, as Chapter 3 will show, there were significant differences between the transfer effects volunteered by teachers and the transfer effects highlighted by the research that has attracted much recent media coverage (see Sharp, 1998 for a critical review of these studies).

The skills which were perceived to be transferable from the arts to other areas of the curriculum included: drawing skills, presentation, performance skills and speaking in front of a group, skills related to group work, communication skills, research skills and accuracy.

These claims for the transfer of skills can be separated into two types: those where transfer was claimed without any reference to examples or evidence, and those where interviewees based their claims on perceived improvements in student performance. The former, in particular, assumes that because common skills are evident across curriculum areas, for example, drawing in biology and art, pupils will be able to make this transfer and use skills developed in the arts within other lessons. The following comment exemplifies the assumption that pupils will be able to *'use art'* when necessary or appropriate in history:

> *If they are doing a history project, they will maybe look at cave painting and maybe in some instances where pupils really cannot communicate in terms of the written language, they have more of an understanding of being able to use art* (head of art).

However, many teachers did focus on their experiences in the classroom, and provided anecdotal evidence to substantiate their claims for the transfer of skills. Interviewees from a range of subject backgrounds described noticeable differences in the work of pupils taking the arts, which they perceived were brought about because of the transfer of skills from the arts to other curriculum areas. Examples from three different curriculum areas were as follows:

> *... if they are good at art, then it does have knock-on effects on presentation. You know, for example, if they are doing a newspaper front page then it will look better, it will be more thought out and they will have got an idea of sort of special awareness of laying out a page* (head of English).

> *I notice in science ... that the spread across of artistic skills into the scientific area, literally in terms of the skill of being able to draw what they see, better ... they are now far more accurate. That is a definite improved skill and that isn't just the higher-ability pupils either* (deputy head).

> *I know that in RE ... I have had feedback from teachers saying to me, you know, 'Oh, we acted out a Christian christening ceremony and it was fascinating to hear them say like "Remember, we must face the audience" and "No, no, no, you are not meant to be on that side. You should be on this side. Now remember, I will freeze and then we will come to life"'. All the things that they have learnt in drama that they are then taking out into other areas and using, which I think is very positive, when they are making these cross-curricular links* (drama and dance teacher).

This last contribution, although still based on teacher perceptions, does suggest that pupils were explicitly making use of techniques developed in drama.

Although claims for transferable skills tended to be specific to individual artforms, some interviewees spoke of the transfer of creativity or thinking skills which went across the arts. This deputy head with a non-arts background discussed the development and then transfer of critical skills (being able to critique work) and problem solving:

> *... it is learning those critical skills, and those are skills that you take across the curriculum. Problem solving, be it a piece of art work, be it trying to make a piece of music from some ideas, or the drama, this is the theme we are working on, it is problem solving, in space and shape and dance ... so there are all those kind of levels of skills and experience that are transferable both across the curriculum in school, but in terms of life skills, as far as I can see.*

A head of expressive arts focused on creative thinking, and the process of investigating, making and recording as common areas of experience in the arts and other subjects:

> *It is learning to think in lots of different ways. Creative thinking I would say is one of the things that they do get from us and all the usual investigating, making, recording. Well yes, we do all those things that you do in other subjects.*

Related to the transfer of creative skills and thinking were references to the transfer of creativity itself, and the transferability of an *'arts-making process'*:

> *I would have thought that creativity in one area of the curriculum must lead to creativity in another area of the curriculum, for example, their linguistic creativity and so on, I think one does lead to the other* (deputy head).

> *... the way that it's not necessarily the first idea that's the best. I mean it's not necessarily a bad thing to ditch 90 per cent of what you've just done and just keep ten per cent and go on. I mean that kind of arts-making process is very transferable, isn't it, to other subjects, to life, to your family? ...* (drama teacher).

Distinguishable from the transfer of skills, many responses also focused on the transferability of knowledge or curriculum content. Some responses (notably from drama, and indicative of the placement of drama within the English curriculum), focused on transfer related to National Curriculum requirements:

> *... particularly in the speaking and listening attainment target, there is a specific reference there to using drama and role play in the teaching of English and in fact all English classrooms should have some drama element* (head of English).

> [I introduced Shakespeare] *specifically through drama in Year 8 so they were used to doing Shakespeare by the time they got to Year 9 where they have to do it for SATs in English ... you would introduce it in a workshop style so that they came with the idea into Year 9 'Oh Shakespeare, goody, goody it's fun, I like Shakespeare'* (drama teacher).

Some arts teachers talked of how their subject area was *'beneficial'* to other areas of the curriculum: for example, drama giving a deeper understanding of characters in English and history:

It brings it to life for them, it takes it off the page ...

For example, in English, if you were this person ... what would you do? Why? You know, when they're reading a novel in history, why did this person do what they did? Why did Henry VIII have his wives executed? I mean, hopefully they would think about that and if then you could go into role and do some drama on that, you know, they do have an amazing ability to think as other people.

A further variant was those teachers who spoke of giving pupils experiences in the arts to support the work done in other subjects. One drama teacher, for example, described work around the theme of war to back up a World War II topic in history, and another suggested that linking drama to every curriculum area was a way forward for drama, with its marginalised place within the National Curriculum:

I like to think of the arts going into every curriculum subject, which is what I try to do. I try to link in what I am doing, you know, to other subjects. I think that really is how drama especially has to go as we are not part of, independently part of, the National Curriculum.

Teachers recognised the potential for cross-curricular themes and topics, but even within the arts themselves, constraints meant that the opportunity to work together could be lost:

Art makes masks; we don't do it at the same time with the same year group ... things that they do in music, I could use in drama. Do you know what I mean? Dance ... does something on the North American Indians. My mask and mime project is on a North American legend, but we don't do it at the same time with the same groups. It is a timetabling restriction and it is also our aim to get ourselves working together, you know (drama teacher).

A final type of response in this sub-category dealing with transfer to other curriculum areas was where teachers spoke of techniques and processes from the arts being used in non-arts lessons. Most common was the use of 'empathy exercises' and role play, for example, acting out red blood cells trying to get through a blocked artery. One drama teacher spoke of trying to encourage teachers to make use of dramatic techniques:

I would like to, say, do an INSET day on how they can use, other subjects can use drama techniques in their lessons. I think there is a natural, inbred fear from other departments when it comes to drama. The idea of having kids walking around talking is, is, you know, seems horrific.

Although wider use of teaching methods and techniques common in the arts was seen as relevant to this 'transfer effects' category, facilitating transfer may not be the intention behind the use of role play and other techniques across the curriculum. It could be that a different rationale — such as motivating pupils, or a school-wide focus on teaching styles — are in operation for those non-arts teachers adopting techniques from the arts. It should be reiterated that in responses claiming transfer of both skills and knowledge from the arts to other curriculum areas, teachers are making claims about perceived transfer. It was not evident to what extent, if any, teachers explicitly made these connections with pupils, or whether pupils perceive this transfer to be happening themselves – this is an area that requires further exploration.

12.4 Facilitates transference of skills/knowledge to work/employability/job /careers.

Drama was particularly associated with this perceived effect, and the following quote sums up this claim:

> ... the other aspect is, of course, the process of it, the learning process, the collaborative process that are transferable skills that you can take anywhere. That is kind of how I start – I don't believe drama and dance to be sort of things that you put on a stage and show. I believe that the whole process of creating anything and working collaboratively, then stepping out and being solo amongst a group, are life skills (dance and drama teacher).

An LEA arts adviser focused on jobs available in the arts (see 12.6), and on the connections between skills developed in the arts and 'what businesses are saying' they want in their employees.

12.5 Encourages involvement in the arts after pupils leave school in unspecified ways.

The following comment summarises this 'unspecified' future involvement sub-category:

> ... my aims in terms of all of it is to get a sort of lifelong thirst for knowledge and enjoyment (headteacher).

12.6 Encourages involvement in the arts after pupils leave school in their careers/work/employment.

An LEA adviser for the arts emphasised the importance of encouraging children to believe that there are jobs in the arts:

> To say to the kids 'Look you can do anything ... you want to be an actor – what a good idea; you know we will help you', not 'Whoa – no jobs in acting'.

Other teachers tended to focus on encouraging pupils to engage in further study in the arts, particularly at art college.

12.7 Encourages involvement in the arts after pupils leave school in their leisure.

This sub-category contained teacher aims for pupils to continue to make music, enjoy reading, and go to dramatic productions and art galleries, no matter what they do as a career:

... it will be with them throughout their lives, because they, if they even do astrophysics, there'll still, wherever they are, there will always be an art gallery where they are, they can always go and spend an afternoon there, it's all around them and hopefully they will take that with them, it's always there. Not even just in the gallery, but all around them wherever (head of art).

B.   EFFECTS ON THE SCHOOL

The effects of arts education on the school were categorised into those focusing on school ethos, the pastoral domain and school image.

13.0   *EFFECTS ON SCHOOL ETHOS*

Numerous responses addressed ways in which the arts contribute to school ethos. Although four sub-categories were devised from the data, distinguishing between an 'adventurous' ethos, a 'positive and enjoyment-oriented' ethos, school pride, and school bonding, in practice it was sometimes difficult to place responses neatly into one of these. Most responses fitted more comfortably into the second sub-category, being claims that the arts help to create a positive and enjoyment-oriented atmosphere in the school.

13.1   Creates adventurous atmosphere/ethos/climate/culture in school.

This sub-category was created to account for responses which focused on the creation of an adventurous ethos or culture in the school, perhaps connected with the risk-taking of creativity. However, although this may be an element of the effect that the arts have on school ethos, most interviewees talked more generally about a *'positive'* school ethos.

13.2   Creates positive and enjoyment-oriented atmosphere and ethos/climate/culture in school, nurtures learning environment.

Most responses focused on the arts as a whole rather than distinguishing between artforms when talking about school ethos.

One stated effect was the philosophy that all can achieve, or, as one deputy head described it, a 'can do it' attitude which began in the arts and permeates the whole school:

> *... these kids may live in one of the most deprived areas in the country, yes; these kids may live in tower blocks, yes; these kids' parents may not have work – that does not mean that they can't achieve. What really happened was that permeated through the rest of the school; it already existed within the arts environment.*

A second aspect was enjoyment, illustrated by this response from a head teacher:

> *I suppose the element of our school aims is the sense of pride and enjoyment, and the arts contribute to both of those – that is our second aim. I believe*

particularly with young people in their teenage years that if they enjoy what they do and they are proud of it, then they are likely to put more time and energy.

Although most responses were not artform-specific, one deputy head made particular mention of the impact drama has on the school:

Drama has a huge input in this school, to actually the whole ethos of the school in that you can express yourself through improvisation, you can explore ideas, you can explore emotions and all sorts of things through drama.

13.3 Encourages pride/self-esteem in a school (which can be identified with by its members).

One response captured much of the character of this outcome:

Pride. I have watched kids walk out of previous performances, previous plays, and seen ... and you can see a tangible sense of 'It is my school and I am proud of it' (deputy head).

Pride was also perceived to be evident in the way that pupils respect and value works of art. This was an aspect mentioned by teachers in one school in particular:

The other thing that I think does come across is that it is very rarely damaged, it is very rarely touched; now a lot of it is sugar paper and yet somehow ... we get no complaints of kids wrecking, touching, ruining in any way any of it, so that is another part of the value system, that they do learn to appreciate that the stuff is somebody's and that it is worth being there.

13.4 Knits/binds the school together, bonding effect.

Another key school effect of the arts was the potential for the arts to bind the school together. Responses tended to address this at a departmental level, with a particular acknowledgement of the role of school productions to encourage involvement from departments across the school. One aspect of this was that the arts departments cooperated on projects; a second aspect was the cross-departmental/faculty involvement in school productions, where, for example, technology does the lighting, science works out special effects, and technology designs tickets and signage.

On a more abstract, less tangible level, the arts were also described as providing a school with a '*soul*' and a '*heartbeat*'.

14.0 EFFECTS ON PASTORAL DOMAIN AND BEHAVIOUR MANAGEMENT

This claimed effect was encapsulated in one sub-category.

14.1 Supports pastoral provision, helps with effective behaviour management, discipline problems.

Some teachers offered comments about specific pupils who have behaviour problems in other subjects, but are not disruptive in the arts. One drama teacher perceived this to be a result of the opportunities for self-expression which exist in the arts:

> ... sometimes it does seem that the kids who are the bad kids in other subjects, because they are the disruptive ones, are the ones who do really well in our subjects because that expression, that freedom of expression, is what they relish and they are away.

Although there were no specific remarks which discussed the issue of behaviour management and the arts at a school rather than a classroom or individual level, as discussed in Category 13, many discussed the positive effect the arts have on school ethos. Some responses included high standards and expectations of behaviour as aspects of a positive school ethos where individuals are valued and value each other.

15.0 EFFECTS ON SCHOOL'S IMAGE

15.1 Promotes the profile/public image of the school, good publicity.

'Parents' were a recurring theme in this sub-category, with the ultimate outcome of good publicity seeming to be that parents would send their children to the school. The arts were perceived to play an important part in this, providing good examination results, impressive visual displays, and high-profile dramatic productions and musical events. These responses from those involved in school management were explicit about the arts 'selling the school':

> ... we have used the arts, of course, to sell the school in a big way. If you are a parent coming to look around the school, yes, you get to see around the art department; you can't avoid it.

> Whenever I bring parents into this particular block, or round the school, they're amazed at the work that goes on here and they are very impressed and I think that probably in some ways makes them want to send their children here, quite honestly. So it's very much something we want, I want; we, as a management team, are very keen to develop, just for the sake of the school rather than anything else. Maintain its popularity.

C.   EFFECTS ON THE COMMUNITY

16.0   *EFFECTS ON PARENTS AND THE COMMUNITY*
Effects of the arts on the community were divided into two sub-categories: parents and the wider community.

16.1   Encourage involvement/support of parents, involvement in school projects, impact on parents.
Teachers commented on the opportunities that arts events provide for parents to become involved in the school, either through direct involvement such as helping at productions, or through attending events as a consumer. One deputy head also described how the inclusion of a dramatic performance (involving a range of pupils) at an evening dealing with solvent abuse encouraged parents to attend.

16.2   Encourage involvement/support of community, involvement in school projects, impact on community.
Key community effects of the arts were perceived to come from pupils performing in the community at primary schools and retirement homes, and school facilities being made available for use by community groups.

One teacher also perceived that the musical horizons of the community as a whole had been broadened by the work of the school music groups.

D.   EFFECTS ON THE MAKING OF ART

17.0   *ART ITSELF AS AN OUTCOME*
This final category was developed to allow for responses which focused on the making of art and art products, which in their own right were seen as outcomes of arts education. However, when analysis took place, there were only a few responses that fitted into this category.

The importance of art works being '*hung on walls*' was mentioned, with one visual art teacher linking the exhibitions with pupils feeling a sense of achievement (see 7.2). Another visual art teacher distinguished between the arts and other areas of the curriculum in terms of product:

> *... after all, if you sit your GCSE maths, are you going to keep your maths book sitting on the mantelpiece at home for the rest of your life? It's very unlikely, but you might keep your picture that you're proud of, or your pot that you made, for years and years and get pleasure from it and a sense of achievement. I mean there is a visual outcome and you can even see your improvement.*

In drama, the longstanding debate between process and product was alluded to by some teachers. Theatrical product was identified as an outcome of drama, although this may not necessarily mean the putting on of a public performance, but more the 'showing' or 'sharing' of work within a lesson. One drama teacher saw product and process as linked, with each enhancing the other:

> *Now, I believe that the product is very valuable and if a child, or anybody, is proud of their product then that feeds back on their process, and then that feeds back into everybody else watching that and how they think about it.*

FREQUENCY OF REFERENCES TO THE DIFFERENT EFFECTS

Whilst the previous section has sought to illustrate the different categories of teachers' claimed effects for arts education, thus far only very broad and vague indications of the relative frequencies for some of the categories have been signalled. To remedy this, this section offers two tables that show the number of references to all the broad categories and the most common of the specific categories. It is important to note that the use of frequencies here makes no pretensions to endow the data with scientifically rigorous and unproblematic quantification, but aims only to provide a general sense of the greater and lesser amounts of citations received for each of the main categories.

One difficulty with collating a numerical representation for each effect was the system of cross-referencing and multiple coding developed to cater for interview responses containing allusions to more than one category. In these situations, only the main effect being referred to has been included in the count. However, multiple references (of a significant nature) to an effect by the same interviewee (but in different places within the interview) have been counted individually to give as accurate an idea of weighting within categories as possible. Two further issues encountered in the analysis should also be noted:

- English was identified in discussion of the arts in only three schools, and dance in four, whereas the other artforms were included in the typology for all five schools; and
- English and dance were also less likely to be mentioned by teachers of other artforms (art, music and drama were more likely to be mentioned by all interviewees).

These two points have meant variable amounts of data were available for each artform.

Table 2.1 Frequency of broad categories		N
7.	Personal development and self-awareness	208
12.	Extrinsic: transfer effects	122
1.	Knowledge and appreciation of artforms/arts	99
5.	Communication and expressive skills	87
10.	Social skills	79
6.	Thinking and creativity skills	76
2.	Knowledge of the social and cultural domain	72
4.	Technical skills in the artforms/arts	62
11.	Intrinsic: well-being effects	53
9.	Awareness of others	34
13.	School ethos	30
16.	Parents, governors and community	27
3.	Knowledge of the affective domain	20
15.	School image	17
8.	Personal skills	10
17.	Art itself	10
14.	Pastoral domain and behaviour	4
	TOTAL	**1010**

Table 2.2 The most frequent specific categories		N
7.2	Fosters self-esteem	88
12.3	Knowledge/skills transfer	71
4.1/6	Technical skills development	62
5.4	Develops expressive skills	57
7.4	Develops whole/balanced person	48
1.1/5	Knowledge of artforms	47
10.1	Team work	44
7.3	Builds self-confidence	43
6.1	Develops thinking skills	43
11.1	Fulfilment, enjoyment, pleasure	39
9.3	Develops empathy, valuing others	32
1.8	Encourages motivation/inspiration	32

Table 2.1 clearly shows that effects relating to pupils' 'personal development and self-awareness' (Category 7) received substantially more references than any other broad category. It received, for example, more nominations than all the direct artform knowledge and technical skills effects (Categories 1 and 4) put together. Table 2.2 shows that the main reasons for the top ranking of this broad category were the high frequencies of three of its constituent specific categories, namely 'fostering self-esteem' (7.2), 'developing whole/balanced person' (7.4) and 'building self-confidence' (7.3). Assuming that these results reflect a consensus of opinion as to the veracity of these effects, it is pertinent to ask whether the potential of the arts to make major contributions to pupils' personal development is fully recognised in schools' whole curriculum policies and in National Curriculum documents.

The emphasis on personal development goes some way to endorse earlier results from a study by Ross and Kamba (1997), who found that, when 38 secondary school teachers were asked to rank five objectives for teaching the arts, '*the development of my pupils' personal qualities (e.g. creativity, self-esteem, self-confidence)*' was afforded top priority. It should be noted, however, that the item presented in their questionnaire included terms which were categorised differently in the typology presented here (e.g. personal 'qualities' and 'creativity'). Consequently, the two sources of data are not completely comparable.

While Table 2.1 shows that 'extrinsic transfer effects' (Category 12) were the second highest broad category, Table 2.2 indicates that this was largely due to the considerable quantity of references to the alleged capacity of the arts to facilitate improvements in performance in other areas of the curriculum through the transference of skills and knowledge acquired in the arts (12.3). As mentioned earlier, disaggregation of these results by artform produced some interesting findings (see Chapter 3).

Looked at from both tables, the direct effects of 'enhanced knowledge and appreciation of artforms/the arts' (Category 1) and 'increased technical skills in the artforms/ the arts' (Category 4) were prevalent amongst teachers' perceptions of the outcomes of arts education. It is perhaps appropriate to point out that if these two categories were combined, their overall score would be higher than that achieved by 'extrinsic transfer effects' (Category 12).

Other effects that were frequently cited included (in rank order) 'communication and expressive skills' (Category 5), 'social skills' (Category 10), principally teamwork (10.1), skills, aptitudes and abilities associated with 'thinking and creativity' (Category 6) and intrinsic effects (Category 11), especially the outcomes of pleasure and fulfilment that can accompany many experiences in the arts.

VARIATIONS BETWEEN SCHOOLS
Having outlined the typology of claimed effects and the frequency of references to them, we now offer a comparative perspective on the extent to which these perceptions varied across the five secondary schools. Each of the artforms is considered in turn.

Since, in most of the schools, only one or two representatives of each artform were interviewed, it was not possible to indicate whether the differences in perceived effects exemplified below were due to variations in individual teachers' ideologies practice or to differences in school policies and approaches. However, given that in many schools, arts-related subjects are taught by only one or two teachers, the findings serve to illustrate the extent to which schools' perspectives and approaches to arts-oriented subjects are heavily dependent on the viewpoints and qualities of the individual teachers employed to mediate the subjects.

As a final word of introduction, it should be stressed that no assumptions are being made about the degree of correspondence between what teachers say their (intended) effects are ('the rhetoric') and what is provided and focused upon in practice ('the reality'). Through the classroom observations of drama, for example, it was noted in some schools that there was a greater emphasis on theatrical techniques than had been expected from the accounts of intended outcomes collected through the interviews with teachers.

Art

There was quite a substantial variation between schools in the range of outcomes that were seen to result from the visual arts and the degree of emphasis placed on them. At one extreme, teachers at one school proposed a wide range of outcomes with emphases on most of them; at the other extreme, another school had few categories with entries, only three of which were given any degree of emphasis.

This latter school stood out as not only proposing very few outcomes from art education, but also generally placing little emphasis on them. Whilst increased self-esteem/sense of achievement was fairly well emphasised, the only other categories to receive any degree of emphasis were self-confidence and, perhaps significantly, enjoyment (this school seemed to value 'straight' enjoyment more than any other school). It was the only school not to mention technical skills and increased awareness of surroundings.

In contrast, the school at the other extreme saw a comparatively wide range of outcomes, many with some or much emphasis. It was conspicuous in the extent to which it emphasised aesthetic judgements/appreciation, and awareness of social and moral issues, and, to a slightly lesser extent, inspiration/motivation. Also much valued or emphasised by this school were awareness of surroundings, technical skills, self-esteem/achievement and confidence (especially due to benefits for pupils whose first language was not English). Some emphasis was also placed on the 'thinking category', and some on understanding oneself, and the creation of positive atmosphere/ethos in school (the only school to mention this); slight emphasis was placed on therapeutic outcomes (again, the only school to cite this), group work and development of the whole personality, which received particular attention at this school.

All schools registered outcomes of increased knowledge, understanding and/or appreciation (Category 1) – though two schools in particular accentuated effects relating to aesthetic judgement-making and increasing motivation in the arts.

Technical skills in the visual arts and awareness of surroundings were recorded in all schools, except the one with a low number of outcomes described above. Interestingly, only two schools linked art to increased awareness of social/moral issues and only one (the school with a wide range of outcomes described above) associated it with the effect of increased understanding of the affective domain. Broadening awareness of cultural traditions and diversity was proposed as an outcome by all schools except one. Notably, all five schools mentioned increased self-esteem/sense of achievement.

Dance
Given that the actual provision of dance showed such significant variations across the five schools – in one school it was not offered at all, some only touched on it in drama, others had specialist dance teachers who were considered to be located within the arts umbrella, though sometimes taught by members of the PE department – it is not surprising that contrasting perceptions of effects were exhibited.

Interestingly, and perhaps significantly for policy-making, interviewees with a general management role rarely referred to effects associated with dance. Dance teachers were usually the only teachers to put forward outcomes from dance education. Moreover, it was noticeable that the specialist dance teachers at two schools could see many more outcomes than the teachers who combined drama and dance.

There were no categories where all the four schools that taught dance universally nominated a particular outcome. However, three schools all proposed outcomes in the physical well-being category and technical skills outcomes – specifically, movement and dance composition skills.

The two schools that provided 'arts-related' dance through dance-drama referred to a comparatively limited range of outcomes. Technical skills were the only outcomes cited by one of these schools, apart from confidence to perform, which was itself linked to performance skills, and also deconstructing skills entered in the thinking and cognitive abilities category. With no reference to technical skills, the second of these schools proposed even fewer dance-related outcomes: empathy (e.g. understanding prejudice through dance) and confidence of movement as an aspect of the physical well-being category.

In contrast, the two schools that offered 'arts-related' dance as a subject in its own right displayed a wider range of perceived effects with greater emphases, including the development of technical skills. One of these schools, for example, placed much emphasis on the appreciation of dance as an artform, as an artform in its own right, and on inspiration/motivation towards dance. The dance teacher at this school was alone in commenting on transfer of skills to other areas of the curriculum, which s/he saw as far ranging (including maths and science). S/he also commented on the opportunity for children to develop an understanding of themselves through dance. The second of these schools also mentioned a broad array of claimed effects, with some distinctive observations and emphases: notably, self-esteem, enjoyment, group work, social skills, challenging taboos, developing acceptance of physical contact, self-expression, increased awareness of the affective domain and enhanced appreciation of cultural diversity.

Drama

There were significant differences in the quantity and type of claimed effects of drama across the five schools. By way of an illustration of the range of these differences, two schools may be compared.

At one end of the continuum, one school was distinctive in the emphasis it afforded to a whole series of perceived outcomes for drama: especially, understanding one's self, self-esteem/achievement, development of the whole person, self-expression, thinking skills, empathy, group work, social skills and the valuing of outcomes relating to understanding of the environment and heightened awareness of feelings. The main categories where this school neither saw many outcomes nor placed much emphasis were the outcomes associated with understanding and appreciation of dramatic form or theatre, and school or community effects.

At the other end of the spectrum, one school limited the emphasis they placed on outcomes to a narrower range of categories: self-esteem, self-confidence and self-expression. It also mentioned creativity/imagination, challenging taboos and sensitivity.

In contrast, a third school especially valued the communication skills, language development and self-confidence outcomes from drama, because of the large proportion of children for whom English was not a first language. It stood alone in seeing drama as being an important contributor to the ethos of the school; it was the only school to mention pride in the school as an outcome; and it was one of only two schools to propose a bonding effect for the school from drama.

All five schools mentioned categories of knowledge, understanding and appreciation of drama/theatre. However, the first school depicted above was least forthcoming in this respect, considering the weight it attached to other categories. Four schools nominated the inspiration and motivation for drama category. Numerous technical skills were identified by three of the schools (including the first and third schools cited above), but two (including the second school cited above) did not refer to them at all. All five schools felt that there were outcomes regarding increased awareness of social and moral issues. The categories of understanding one's self, self-esteem/achievement, self-confidence, and the development of personality were generally highly valued outcomes. There was also a consensus among drama teachers in all five schools that drama contributed significantly to many other areas of the curriculum through the transference of skills.

English

As with other artforms, the three schools where heads of English were interviewed differed in the number and type of outcomes identified and emphasised. The school that volunteered the widest range of effects from English teaching gave particular emphasis to understanding and analysis of literature, understanding and awareness of the cultural/social world and surroundings, including social and moral issues, technical skills, and creativity. Technical skills were seen as crucially important foundations for other outcomes such as enabling creativity. Notably, this school was the only one to mention self-expression, heightened awareness of feelings/emotions, and the intrinsic outcomes of personal enjoyment and fulfilment.

By way of comparison, the school where the smallest number of outcomes was proposed only accentuated the broadening cultural horizons. It was the only school to mention communication, group work and the development of empathy. Falling between these schools, as far as range and number of outcomes suggested was concerned, the third emphasised the development of critical judgements and inspiration regarding literature, including the continued involvement after school, particularly with respect to reading. Creativity was also emphasised. This school was alone in referring to a sense of achievement, the development of language and discussion skills, and involvement after school.

The only specific outcome mentioned in all three schools was the growth in empathy and the valuing of others category (9.3). Two schools, however, attached considerable emphasis to the categories for increased knowledge, understanding and appreciation of literature.

Music
Perceptions about the range of outcomes produced by music education, as well as the emphases attached to them, varied appreciably between the schools. At the most comprehensive end of the spectrum, one school viewed the effect of music to be extremely wide ranging and often very influential in its alleged impact. The school was exceptional for the importance it placed on the sets of categories relating to personal development, to knowledge, understanding and appreciation of music, and to the development of social skills. Added emphasis was devoted to the individual categories of self-esteem/achievement and group work. It was the only school to mention organisational skills, sensitivity, and the fostering of a positive atmosphere in school.

In contrast, the range of effects posited by a school at the other end of the spectrum was relatively small and very little prominence was placed on those that were. The only categories to receive any emphasis were the nurturing of self-esteem/achievement and, perhaps, the development of the whole personality. It was the only school not to allude to inspiration and motivation for music as an outcome.

A third school displayed another configuration of claimed effects. Although exhibiting the smallest range of outcomes, certain categories were depicted in greater detail. The effect of self-expression was much valued; emphasis was also placed on technical skills and, to a slightly lesser extent, on enjoyment. Technical skills were seen as prerequisites for self-expression, knowledge and understanding of music, and for enjoyment. This school stood out markedly from the other schools in so far as it emphasised expressive effects, and in addition, it was the only school to mention improved performance through behaviour management outcomes from music.

Technical skills in music were referred to in all of the schools and accentuated in three of them. All five schools saw the intrinsic gains of enjoyment/fulfilment as being produced by music.

Overview of school variations

The comparisons offered above revealed that none of the schools demonstrated a propensity to identify the richest and most comprehensive array of perceived effects in all of the artforms. Some schools seemed 'strong' in certain artforms and 'weaker' in others. Although judgements are difficult to make with confidence, it would appear that each of the five schools had at least one of the artforms where the accounts offered of the effects were among the most detailed and widest-ranging portrayals.

Most significantly, it appeared that, to varying extents in different artforms, different schools and/or teachers may be attempting to achieve different effects in their teaching of what is assumed to be the same 'subject'. This point, if confirmed, would have major implications for any examination of the 'effectiveness' of teaching in the arts. It could mean that evaluations of effectiveness need to be based on the outcomes identified by individual teachers as their intended goals. Alternatively, it raises the crucial question, for example, of whether 'effectiveness' is defined as the teacher's ability to achieve his or her intended outcomes, no matter how narrow, or as the ability to achieve the comprehensive range of outcomes typically attributed to the subject by others. Is a broad selection and prioritisation of the intended effects of a particular artform an essential criterion for evaluating effectiveness in the teaching of it?

CONCLUSION

In this chapter, we have attempted to initiate work on the project's first aim by setting out a typology of the claimed effects for arts education, according to the perceptions of teachers interviewed in the five secondary schools. The sub-categories that comprise the typology have been outlined and illustrated. Additionally, the chapter has offered summaries of initial analyses of how the perceived outcomes varied between schools.

It is noteworthy that the typology encompassed a broader and more multifaceted array of desirable outcomes for arts education than that currently codified in the National Curriculum Orders for arts-related subjects at key stages 3 and 4. Although the latter contain references to the enjoyment of art (11.1), the awareness of cultural heritage (2.1) and the expression of ideas (5.4), in the main they tend to be limited to Categories 1 and 4, namely increasing knowledge, understanding and appreciation of the artforms and development in their technical skills.

Throughout the chapter, it has been emphasised that the outcome categories, like the material upon which they are based, are restricted to the status of 'claimed' or 'purported' effects. In fact, in many cases, it was found that the perceptions of teachers represented intended outcomes or aims rather than claimed effects. For the purposes of this analysis, perceived outcomes and intended outcomes have not been differentiated, partly because most interviewees were not predisposed to distinguishing the two and partly because, even for perceived effects, the evidence to support the claims was at best anecdotal. Although the fact that several teachers, to some extent at least, independently corroborated several arts-related outcomes lends some support for their veracity, it remains possible that the community of arts educators collectively mis-recognise or inflate the benefits and effects of the educational provision they wholeheartedly subscribe to and seek to advance. The sceptical response to the contributions described in this chapter is likely to be 'Well, they would say that, wouldn't they'?

This raises one of the biggest challenges facing the study (and, perhaps, arts education in general): having proposed a typology of purported effects, what valid and reliable evidence can be garnered to substantiate these claims? In Phase 1 of the study, two different strategies were used to address this question: an exploratory examination of pupils' perceptions of the effects of arts education (see Chapter 4) and a secondary-data analysis of possible relationships between studying arts-related subjects at key stage 4 and GCSE performance (see Chapter 5). First, however, the following chapter discusses variations in teachers' perceptions of the effects, according to different artforms.

3. HOW THE PERCEIVED EFFECTS VARIED BETWEEN ARTFORMS

INTRODUCTION

This chapter elaborates upon the typology described in Chapter 2 by focusing on variations between artforms in the claims made for the effects of arts education on pupils, the school, the community and the making of art. Again based on responses from 52 staff interviews in the five case study secondary schools, the chapter explores differences in frequency of claims for effects, and variations in the nature of responses, that is differences in emphasis or differences in the ways in which the effect is perceived to function within the artform.

The numerical data presented in the tables throughout this chapter were arrived at through the same processes as those described in the previous chapter – their primary aim here being to enhance analysis of the typology of claimed effects from the perspective of variations by artform.

DIFFERENCES IN THE FREQUENCY OF CLAIMED EFFECTS

Table 3.1 shows the frequency of claims by artform for the 12 broad categories of effects on pupils, the three broad categories for school effects, and the effects on the community and art itself.

'The arts' were often referred to collectively, and in fact, attracted the most mentions in 11 out of the 17 broad categories. However, leaving aside collective references to the arts, visual art and drama were more evident than music. Visual art was dominant in categories involving knowledge and understanding (principally, Categories 1 and 2), whereas drama stood out in categories concerned with relating to others (Categories 9 and 10), and in the development of communication skills (Category 5). Although music was cited marginally more often for the development of technical skills (Category 4) and claims for intrinsic, well-being effects (Category 11), in light of the caveat regarding the status of frequencies, this difference is negligible.

Dance and English are represented to varying degrees across the 12 claimed effects on pupils, but are noticeably absent from effects on the school and community. Indeed, for school and community effects, the arts were much more likely to be referred to collectively, although visual art, music and drama did receive some specific mentions.

For many broad categories, variations only become apparent in analysis of the specific categories contained within them. This chapter now moves on to explore these variations by artform in greater depth.

Table 3.1   Differences by artform in frequency of claimed effects (broad categories)

	Effect (broad categories)	Art (visual)	Dance	Drama	English	Music	The Arts
A. Effects on pupils	1.0 Knowledge and appreciation of artforms/the arts	23	5	16	8	18	29
	2.0 Knowledge of the social & cultural domain	28	1	11	8	3	21
	3.0 Knowledge of the affective domain	1		6	1	2	10
	4.0 Technical skills in the artform/arts	17	3	15	2	20	5
	5.0 Communication & expressive skills	12	1	35	3	5	31
	6.0 Thinking & creativity skills	16	2	15	6	6	31
	7.0 Personal development & self-awareness	42	3	56	3	30	74
	8.0 Personal skills	3		2		1	4
	9.0 Awareness of others	3	1	15	3	2	10
	10.0 Social skills	3	4	26		19	27
	11.0 Intrinsic: well-being effects	9	7	4	1	13	19
	12.0 Extrinsic: transfer effects	31	1	30	4	12	44
B. School effects	13.0 School ethos	2		5		1	22
	14.0 Pastoral domain and behaviour			2		2	
	15.0 School image	3		2		1	11
C. Community effects	16.0 Parents, governors and community	3		5		8	11
D. Art as product	17.0 Art itself	3		4			3
	TOTAL	199	28	249	39	143	352

VARIATIONS IN SPECIFIC CATEGORY EFFECTS

A.   EFFECTS ON PUPILS

1.0   *KNOWLEDGE, UNDERSTANDING AND APPRECIATION OF THE ARTS AND INDIVIDUAL ARTFORMS*

Table 3.2   Differences by artform for Category 1

	Effect (specific categories)	Art (visual)	Dance	Drama	English	Music	The Arts
1.1 1.5	Knowledge and understanding of the artform	14	4	11	7	11	
1.6	Fosters perceptions of cross-arts					1	5
1.7	Extends appreciation of the arts			1			14
1.8	Encourages motivation & inspiration in the artform	9	1	4	1	6	10

Some interesting differences between artforms emerged in claims for effects relating to increases in knowledge and understanding of the artforms (1.1-1.5). Particularly marked was the scarcity of claims for dance. Although one teacher did describe pupils using the language of dance such as '*body shapes*' and '*travelling*', and another stated an aim as '*... to make people more aware, make people more aware of dance in its own right*', there was no mention of the development of critical skills or the making of aesthetic judgements about dance similar to those, for example, associated with the visual arts. An LEA arts adviser emphasised the importance of pupils having experiences in dance which '*... can help them to understand the conventions of dance, of how dance actually works ...*', but the absence of claims related to understanding and making judgements about dance performances suggests that this may not be occurring in teacher aims or practice. Again, one possible reason for this is the marginalised status of dance in the curriculum, where pupils have less time to experience dance than the other artforms, and often experience it as a module of physical education.

Leaving aside dance, there was no notable variation in the frequency of claims for effects related to knowledge, understanding and appreciation for the other artforms (although English had fewer responses, it was proportionately well-represented in relation to the overall number of responses for English).

However, a divergence in emphasis did emerge. Art and drama teachers tended to focus on enhancing critical skills, developing language associated with the artform, and making aesthetic judgements about works of art or dramatic performances. There was an emphasis in responses on pupils interpreting and evaluating their own work and that of others. Responding critically to texts and commenting on others' work was also seen as an important effect within English.

In contrast, music teachers tended to focus more on pupils being able to '*appreciate*' and enjoy music. Although there was recognition that this appreciation is enhanced by, or even dependent on, greater understanding of music, there were few references to the development of critical skills, evaluation and aesthetic judgement-making.

Another interesting point was that claims for increasing knowledge and understanding of the historical context of the artform were notably absent from anything but visual art. This is perhaps due to the established place of art within the school curriculum and the existence of the field of 'art history' in its own right.

The claim that teaching the arts encourages a sense of inspiration in the artform (1.8) was made for visual art more than for other artforms, with emphasis placed on the capacity for school art displays and exhibitions to raise the aspirations and standards of those viewing them. Although one deputy head suggested that outside performers could raise aspirations for pupils, public events in other artforms – drama, music or dance performances – did not appear to be endowed with the same potential for affecting others as public events in visual art.

2.0 *KNOWLEDGE AND UNDERSTANDING OF THE SOCIAL AND CULTURAL DOMAIN*

Table 3.3   Differences by artform for Category 2

	Effect (specific categories)	Art (visual)	Dance	Drama	English	Music	The Arts
2.1	Develops knowledge of cultural traditions, multicultural insights	8	1		5	3	9
2.2	Awareness of pupils' surroundings	14		1	2		7
2.3	Awareness of social and moral issues	6		10	1		5

Teachers in most artforms made claims about the arts broadening horizons and developing understanding of cultural traditions (2.1). A particular aspect to emerge in the data was multiculturalism and cultural diversity: that pupils could experience the music, visual art, dance and literature of other cultures, and therefore gain a greater understanding of these cultures. Interestingly, there were no responses relating to drama that fitted this category. Visual art teachers tended to focus more on pupils appreciating the work of different artists and art from other countries, rather than express aims relating to developing understandings of cultural diversity.

An interesting distinction also came in the use of the term 'culture'. Within the context of broadening horizons, some teachers spoke of what could be termed 'high culture', and saw the arts as raising the awareness of cultural perspectives through theatre trips and concerts. This use of culture was particularly related to English.

Responses also addressed ways in which the arts can promote awareness of pupils' surroundings and their place within them (2.2). Visual awareness, through art education, was mentioned particularly frequently:

> *I suppose in essence what we are trying to do is to sensitise individuals to their environment and to their surroundings – things that they see, touch and experience* (ex head of art).

> *... seeing this world accurately is good visual art education* (deputy head).

Drama, on the other hand, was dominant in 2.3 – it was seen as an artform where pupils could develop awareness of society through exploration of issues:

> *I know in drama they do a lot of cultural problems so that you've got a lot of awareness of society; they do real life situations which is really good* (head of music).

One visual art teacher also talked about the issues that could be discussed in art lessons; she described as '*perfect occasions*' those times when everyone is on-task and one conversation can go on for the whole group as they work on their art. This is an aspect of arts education related to teacher-pupil relationships and general education rather than to the visual art curriculum itself.

3.0   *KNOWLEDGE AND AWARENESS OF THE AFFECTIVE DOMAIN*

Table 3.4   Differences by artform for Category 3

Effect (specific categories)	Art (visual)	Dance	Drama	English	Music	The Arts
3.0 Knowledge of the affective domain	1		6	1	2	10

Claims that the arts develop a heightened awareness of the world of feelings and emotions (3.0) were made for the arts generally, and specifically for drama. The arts were seen to provide opportunities for pupils to explore their own feelings and those of others, and drama techniques such as mime were suggested as contributing to achieve this effect.

4.0   *TECHNICAL SKILLS IN THE ARTFORMS/ARTS*

Table 3.5   Differences by artform for Category 4

Effect (specific categories)	Art (visual)	Dance	Drama	English	Music	The Arts
4.0 Technical skills in the artform/arts	17	3	15	2	20	5

Claims about effects relating to developments in technical skills and capabilities were made for all artforms, but were stronger for drama, music and visual art.

Technical skills were specific to each artform: (by way of illustration) secretarial skills in English; movement skills and coordination in dance; observational skills, colour mixing and developing tonal drawing in visual art; improvisation, role and mime in drama; and developing rhythm and auditory ability in music. However, there were differences between teachers (rather than artforms) for the types of skills emphasised, and the extent to which these were seen to be a critical element of education in the arts. A particular divergence came in drama between an emphasis on performance-based theatre skills or on dramatic processes or techniques. This is indicative of the longstanding product-process debate.

Despite technical skills being specific to artforms, a crucial point which emerged from responses across the arts was the importance of pupils gaining technical skills to enable them to be creative and express themselves through the artform. Teachers from all artforms talked of '*creating an atmosphere*', where pupils could be creative, use their imagination, and try things out.

Performance skills were also included by teachers of music, dance and drama. These were closely related to the 'develops confidence' effect.

5.0   *COMMUNICATION AND EXPRESSIVE SKILLS*

Table 3.6   Differences by artform for Category 5

	Effect (specific categories)	Art (visual)	Dance	Drama	English	Music	The Arts
5.1	Develops communication skills	2		7	1		5
5.2	Encourages development of language, eloquence			8			
5.3	Develops listening skills			3			4
5.4	Develops expressive skills, self-expression	10	1	17	2	5	22

Drama was particularly dominant for effects related to communication, with responses for all specific categories (communication skills, development of language, listening skills and expressive skills). Drama was perceived more than other artforms to provide opportunities for pupils to communicate and relate to other people, and to engage with the world:

> *I see drama as a means of people engaging with the world around them ...*
> *and in that way hopefully develop them to analyse and communicate*
> *interactively with what is around them, and to question ... it has become*
> *more important as the world around the kids has become more complex;*
> *their ability to engage in, receive, question and communicate in an*
> *intelligible way is becoming more and more important* (drama teacher).

More specific than the development of general communication skills, a claimed effect of drama was the development of language and skills of delivery, such as the ability to speak in front of a group with clarity (5.2), and the development of listening skills (5.3).

The development of expressive skills enabling pupils to make statements about themselves and their world (5.4) was an effect frequently claimed for all artforms, although many teachers spoke about this in terms of the arts generally, rather than their own subject area. There was an emphasis on the arts as being particularly valuable for pupils for whom English is not a first language or for less academically able pupils, as they provide a means of communication not based on writing. This could suggest that many interviewees were not including English as an artform in this context – indeed, in the responses for this effect from English teachers, there was not a focus on second language pupils or on the less academic – one teacher talked about verbal expression, the other on using descriptive language to express ideas in creative writing.

A further variation by artform was in references to the expression of 'ideas' or 'feelings'. In drama and visual art, there were references to both. Mentions of this effect for music and dance, however, focused on feelings, for example dance providing an opportunity for pupils to let go of some of their emotions without being aggressive. In English, there was an emphasis solely on the expression of ideas.

Another interesting point to emerge in this category was the recognition that the artforms themselves provide distinct means of self-expression, and that pupils often display aptitude or interest in a particular artform. One teacher described a desired outcome being for pupils *'to be able to feel that they can – if not express themselves in the way that they feel they would like in one format – do it elsewhere'* (head of Welsh).

6.0   *THINKING SKILLS AND CREATIVITY*

Table 3.7   Differences by artform for Category 6

	Effect (specific categories)	Art (visual)	Dance	Drama	English	Music	The Arts
6.1	Develops thinking skills; problem-solving skills; independent thinking	8	1	13	1	5	20
6.2	Develops creativity	8	1	2	5	1	11

Claims about effects relating to thought processes, developing logical argument, representing the world mentally and problem-solving (6.1) were made to some extent for all artforms, but they emerged particularly with reference to drama and the arts collectively. Drama was seen to achieve this effect through both content and process, that is, pupils thinking through issues and working with techniques such as thought tracking, where one person is doing the action while another acts as their thoughts.

Responses from drama, visual art and dance touched on deconstruction, through which pupils are encouraged to think about how a piece of work is put together. One head of music also distinguished between the emotional and cognitive aspects of music:

> *... the more mechanical nature of music, how is it put together and almost the more formal teaching of music, forget this portraying of emotion, so yes, there is that in it as well. If you look at formal music teaching, formal harmony a lot of it is cognitive ...*

All artforms were perceived to develop creativity (6.2), although interestingly, in contrast to the other categories for this effect, this was not strongly expressed with regard to drama. It was also negligible for dance and music. Whilst the compositional element within the National Curriculum for music was referred to in teacher interviews, it may be that this is associated more with effects such as the development of technical skills, and pupils working together in groups, than with the development of creativity. This would appear consistent with the emphasis placed on technical skills in music, where it is seen that pupils need to gain technical skills to enable them to be creative.

English and visual art teachers in particular spoke about the role of the teacher in providing pupils with the opportunities to produce art work or creative writing through processes of exploration and experimentation, and linked this to pupil confidence:

> *Well, I think it can develop children, pupils, to give them a sense of their surroundings – a sense of self-confidence as well – which I think is very important. Always try and get across there's no right or wrongs; there's always questions and you've got to answer them in your own way. So it's quite a venture of self-discovery, sometimes, doing a piece of art work and we can all draw the same objects in the centre of the room but come out with a totally different piece of work – and that's fine* (head of art).

> *I think that the emphasis is to try and get them to become not afraid of trying different things, to be confident* (head of English).

As discussed earlier in this chapter, creativity was also connected with technical skills – pupils were seen to need a grounding in artform-specific technical skills to enable them to express themselves and be creative.

7.0   *PERSONAL DEVELOPMENT AND SELF-AWARENESS*

Table 3.8   Differences by artform for Category 7

	Effect (specific categories)	Art (visual)	Dance	Drama	English	Music	The Arts
7.1	Develops an understanding of one's self, self-awareness	8		7		1	12
7.2	Fosters self-esteem	20	2	21	1	18	26
7.3	Builds self-confidence	9	1	14	1	6	13
7.4	Develops whole/balanced person	5		14	1	5	23

Category 7 constituted a major set of effects claimed for the arts, and was particularly evident in music, visual art and drama. From the single artforms, drama received the largest number of responses in this broad category; this is the result of more references to the developing confidence effect (7.3) and to the development of the 'whole person' (7.4).

For 7.1 (developing an understanding of one's self), there was a focus in drama on pupils having the opportunity to explore issues and in so doing discover things about themselves. In visual art, the focus of teacher responses was more on pupils having the opportunity to produce unique pieces of work and develop individuality through this.

There were multiple references to the arts fostering self-esteem and confidence (7.2 and 7.3). There were almost equal responses for visual art, drama and music with regard to the fostering self-esteem effect, and again there was a particular emphasis on the pupils who do not achieve so highly in other curriculum areas but gain a sense of achievement through their arts participation. Self-esteem and confidence were seen to be enhanced through successful public displays such as drama performances and art exhibitions, as well as from the sense of achievement that individual pupils gain from classroom-based or private work. One teacher, who emphasised the importance of performance in developing confidence, distinguished between the artforms:

> *I'd say that probably the drama creates probably more self-confidence than the other two* [art and music] *and the visual arts creates maybe a little less confidence and maybe music in the middle is a combination of the two. I mean in music you have the introspective creative individual kind of operation which is similar maybe to drawing or to exploring something visually, but also it demands quite often an element of performance which then takes it towards the drama side, where people work together to create a performance* (head of Welsh).

Whilst all artforms were seen to develop self-confidence to some extent, drama was dominant here, particularly in the sub-group of responses labelled 'develops confidence – unspecified'. Drama, music and dance all had references to building confidence in performing.

8.0 *DEVELOPS PERSONAL SKILLS*

Table 3.9   Differences by artform for Category 8

	Effect (specific categories)	Art (visual)	Dance	Drama	English	Music	The Arts
8.1	Develops sense of responsibility						2
8.2	Enhances organisational skills					1	1
8.3	Develops independence and autonomy	3		2			1

There were few responses for the personal skills effect from any artforms, or for the arts collectively.

9.0 *AWARENESS OF OTHERS*

Table 3.10   Differences by artform for Category 9

	Effect (specific categories)	Art (visual)	Dance	Drama	English	Music	The Arts
9.1	Encourages tolerance						1
9.2	Develops sensitivity			1			
9.3	Develops empathy, valuing others	3	1	14	3	2	9

The only sub-category of note for this effect was 9.3, developing empathy and valuing others. Although all artforms were evident, this effect was particularly prevalent in responses relating to drama.

The two aspects included in this sub-category (being empathetic or valuing others) provided an interesting contrast by artform. Responses for English and drama focused on pupils developing empathy through seeing things from other perspectives. For English, this was related to process factors – discussion groups and pupils working together – and to content – the themes within English which address tolerance. Drama teachers also talked in terms of process and content, and again techniques (thought tracking and going into role) were important:

> *Suddenly they really get inside the head of somebody else. And can understand that situation through the eyes of somebody else ...*

> *... having to play the racist, having to play the person who doesn't have the feelings that you have. You know, that is something they don't get the chance to do. So, you know, it's a really valuable thing to be able to play those opinions, play that character without having to answer really for their, for what they said after you come out of role* (drama teacher).

In contrast, for visual art and music, responses related to pupils respecting and appreciating the work of other pupils: '... *music necessitates listening to what others have created, patiently and politely*' (head of Upper School & music teacher).

10.0   *SOCIAL SKILLS*

Table 3.11   Differences by artform for Category 10

	Effect (specific categories)	Art (visual)	Dance	Drama	English	Music	The Arts
10.1	Teamwork	2	1	13		13	15
10.2	Develops social skills	1	2	12		3	9
10.3	Challenges taboos		1	1			
10.4	Improves communication between teachers, pupils					3	3

Improvement in the capacity to work in a group (10.1) was recognised in all artforms, excluding English. This effect was expressed particularly in regard to drama and music. Whilst visual art teachers spoke of providing opportunities for pupils to work together and share ideas, responses from music, dance and drama teachers give the impression that group work plays a different role in their teaching. 'The group' is often central to the creation of a performance or composition:

> *... you can't actually do drama on your own ...* (drama teacher).

> *... they have to learn to work with others. I think also that the whole working with other people, touching other people, holding other people, supporting*

*other people – you know having to be aware of where someone else is in the
room because it affects where you are ...* (dance teacher).

It is interesting to place frequencies of response for 5.1-5.3 (communication skills)
alongside those for 10.1 (teamwork). Whilst both emerged as strong effects for drama
(that is, drama was perceived to develop communication and the ability to work in a
group), for music this relationship was different. In music, claims for developing
communication skills were not made. However, music still occurred frequently in this
related effect in Category 10. This suggests that although music was seen to provide
opportunities for pupils to develop teamwork skills through composing and
performing in groups, these experiences were not perceived to be developing the skills
of communication.

Drama was also to the fore in the development of social skills (10.2), where there was
an emphasis on drama having this effect because of the opportunities for pupils to
interact with others in lessons, and because of the themes addressed, which often deal
with people in social situations.

For dance and drama, an aim for two male teachers was challenging taboos (10.3) and
the breaking down of stereotypes based on gender:

> *It is all developing good social skills, especially, again, with the boys, who
> just don't hug each other. It has sort of developed that I am not going to be
> scared to touch another person of the same sex* (dance teacher).

Another aspect of social skills development was the development of a different
relationship between teacher and pupil (10.4). This was mentioned particularly in
connection with music:

> *When you step out of role and you become collaborators in a project, you are
> still a teacher, but you are sharing those things together with the kids and
> that is vitally important for the kids to see that, to experience that* (deputy
> head).

11.0   *INTRINSIC: WELL-BEING EFFECTS*

Table 3.12   Differences by artform for Category 11

	Effect (specific categories)	Art (visual)	Dance	Drama	English	Music	The Arts
11.1	Fulfilment, enjoyment, pleasure	6	2	4	1	10	16
11.2	Therapeutic outcomes	3				3	3
11.3	Enhances physical health		5				

Claims about effects relating to improvements in general well-being were made for all
artforms. There was a particular emphasis on enjoyment (11.1), with arts participation
described as producing '*a buzz*' and an adrenaline rush (see Harland *et al.*, 1995).
Some staff saw music and visual art as being of therapeutic value and providing a
means of release (11.2). Dance was the only artform linked with the enhancement of

73

physical health and fitness (11.3), and this sub-category was the major effect claimed for dance.

12.0 *EXTRINSIC: TRANSFER EFFECTS*

Table 3.13   Differences by artform for Category 12

	Effect (specific categories)	Art (visual)	Dance	Drama	English	Music	The Arts
12.1	Improves performance in other curriculum areas — unspecified					3	6
12.2	Improves performance in other curriculum areas — motivation, behaviour, attitudes	5					7
12.3	Knowledge/skills transfer	20	1	26	3	5	16
12.4	Transferability to employability/work	1		2			7
12.5	Encourages post-school arts involvement — unspecified				1	1	3
12.6	Encourages post-school arts involvement — employment	4		1		1	4
12.7	Encourages post-school arts involvement — leisure	1		1		2	1

There were some references in music to unspecified transfer effects – '*Music is such a fantastic educational tool*' (music teacher) – and in visual art to improved school performance as a result of better motivation, behaviour and attitudes:

> *... there's a teapot made of a flower from a lad in GCSE and that is probably his finest achievement in this school and he's done that through art. But what that's given him is dignity, which has come to other areas of the school ...* (head).

However, a major claimed effect in this category, and indeed across all specific categories, was the transfer of knowledge and skills into other areas of the curriculum. A number of differences by artform also emerged for this effect. Immediately obvious is that although each artform is evident, visual art and drama are particularly dominant – indeed, both artforms have more references for this effect than do the arts collectively.

Of particular note is the limited number of claims for improved performance in other curriculum areas made for music. As discussed in Chapter 5, music has been the main focus for studies on transfer effects (Sharp, 1998), and although the one reference to research by an arts teacher in the case study schools was from a head of music, this did not seem to be being claimed in terms of their own music teaching. Chapter 5 also presents some initial analysis of possible relationships between taking arts courses at key stage 4 and general GCSE academic attainment, and without making claims of causality, suggests a positive association between studying music and core subject GCSE performance. In light of this, it is interesting that the case study data presented here does not indicate that teachers of music and other staff (notably senior management) see transfer of knowledge or skills as a key effect of music education. Indeed, in contrast to the attention given to music in previous research and recent media coverage, teachers were more likely to identify transfer effects in drama and visual art than in music.

In terms of the type of transfer, differences were evident between the claims made for visual art and those for drama. Broadly speaking, with regard to visual art, teachers made claims for the transfer of skills such as drawing, accuracy, the setting out of work and presentation to other areas of the curriculum, whilst, with regard to drama, teachers focused on knowledge and curriculum content. Teachers spoke of drama's explicit curriculum links (with health education, personal and social education and National Curriculum English requirements), and of drama reinforcing work done in other areas: for example, war could be a theme for history and drama. Responses for drama also highlighted the adoption of drama techniques by teachers in other areas of the curriculum: for example, the use of role play and thought tracking in history. In schools where this occurs, pupils may be being given opportunities to transfer skills used in drama to support their learning in other curriculum areas. However, as suggested in discussion of this effect in Chapter 2, there is no evidence that teachers are explicit about this transferability of skills or knowledge, and pupils may not be making these connections themselves.

Although a connection between music and mathematics is often perceived to be evident, there was only fleeting reference to this from interviewees – the mathematical precision required in music, and the rhythmic, numerical basis to dance. Transference of skills claims for English focused on communication aspects, such as speaking and listening: '*It should help with general sort of communication, confidence and ability to present logical arguments*' (head of English).

The effects of arts involvement were also seen to extend beyond a pupil's time at school, either through the transference of skills or knowledge into the workplace (12.4) or through continued involvement in the arts as an adult through a career or leisure activities (12.5-12.7). While a case for the arts was often put forward with reference to these post-school transfer effects, there was little variation by artform. The only exception was the emphasis on further or higher education courses and careers leading from visual art.

B.   EFFECTS ON THE SCHOOL

Table 3.14   Differences by artform for Categories 13, 14 and 15

	Effect	Art (visual)	Dance	Drama	English	Music	The Arts
13.0	School ethos	2		5		1	22
14.0	Pastoral domain and behaviour			2		2	
15.0	School image	3		2		1	11

The arts tended to be spoken of collectively for their contribution to a positive ethos or climate in the school (13.0), although visual art, drama and music were also mentioned specifically. English and dance were not specified at all. One head of art mentioned the significance of having a head who appreciates the importance of the arts, and stated: '*I've always said, always believed that a strong art department is a strong school.*'

In one school, drama was perceived to contribute to a positive ethos by providing opportunities for emotions to be explored, and it was claimed that drama techniques were used in assemblies. In visual art, displays were perceived to contribute to the ethos as part of the '*value system*' where pupils appreciate and respect the work, and by providing a focus for interaction between pupils.

Another claimed effect for the arts was that they encourage pride in the school: '*I have watched kids walk out of previous performances, previous plays ... and you can see a tangible sense of "It is my school and I am proud of it"*' (deputy head). Arts productions were also seen to bind the school together through involvement from multiple departments, where, for example, the technology classes help with stage lighting and tickets are produced in IT. Drama was mentioned specifically with regard to a claim of 'bonding', where a sense of togetherness is encouraged.

There were minimal mentions of drama and music having an effect on the pastoral domain and behaviour (14.0). These references tended to refer to an individual pupil level rather than suggesting that the effect operated at the level of the school.

The effect of the arts on school image (15.0) was noted, particularly by interviewees involved in school management. Language such as '*public relations*', '*reputation*', and '*a showcase for the school*' was used; as one head said, '*... it's very much something we want, I want, we, as a management team are very keen to develop, just for the sake of the school rather than anything else*'. Teachers of visual art, music and drama also talked about the effect that '*success*' in their subject areas can have on school image. There was an emphasis on public displays of the arts (art exhibitions and wall displays, musical events and dramatic productions) and on achievement:

> *At its crudest, when you are getting 93 per cent A to Cs in art and you are able to say that to parents, you are able to inspire parents to send their daughters here to get the balanced intake* (deputy head).

One possibility for the absence of dance for this effect may be that it is not examinable in the same way as drama, music and art, and cannot therefore be held up as an indication of school success.

There appears to be an expectation that 'entertainment' will be provided for school occasions, but, as the following extract from an interview with a music teacher suggests, participation in events moves beyond entertainment, and serves other purposes in the school. A distinction is also drawn between artforms, in the valuing of performance, with a suggestion as to why effects on school image are not claimed for English:

> *It's what people see ... Year 6 parents' evening. What do they want? They want music, because it shows off, shows off what you can do, what the school*

is about. You can't put a piece of English on the stage. Any event that goes on for parents, they always want music (head of music).

Dance and English were absent from all mention of effects on the school, and although this is no doubt partly a result of the fewer mentions of these subjects overall, it may also suggest that these two subjects hold different places within the school curriculum relative to the more established arts subjects (visual art, drama and music). Dance is not a stand-alone National Curriculum subject, and tends to be situated within physical education. English, in contrast to dance, occupies a core position within the curriculum, but generally serves other functions within the school rather than one related to its links with the arts.

C.   EFFECTS ON THE COMMUNITY

Alongside the effect of the arts on school image, the arts were also seen to be encouraging the involvement of parents and the wider community in the school (see Table 3.1). Although again the arts were often spoken of collectively, one deputy head described how a parents' evening on problems with solvents was enhanced by a dramatic production confronting the issue:

> *It was absolutely fantastic and I just don't think that we would easily have got that mix of people without that input, because it is having an entertainment, putting on an entertainment like that, but looking at some quite serious issues.*

Community involvement was claimed to be enhanced by the arts in schools where facilities were used by the wider community, and by music and drama groups taking performances to local schools and other community locations. One deputy head believed that the band at the school had widened horizons for the community as a whole:

> *The big band connection that we have had here for years and years – that has opened up horizons that* [town] *never thought it had horizons for. Not just, as I said, in terms of the high level of skill that they have reached musically, but as I say, just to open a perspective that didn't exist.*

D.   EFFECTS ON THE MAKING OF ART

Few responses were claims about effects on art itself as an outcome. As indicated in Table 3.1, those that *were* focused on the importance of the performance or product in drama and visual art.

OVERVIEW OF ARTFORM VARIATIONS

Differences by artform were evident in terms of variation in the significance attached to each effect, differences in emphasis, and different perceptions of how the effect functioned. The ranking of specific effects on pupils for each artform is summarised below.

Drama

> *Transfer of knowledge and skills (12.3)*
>
> *Fosters self-esteem (7.2)*
>
> *Develops expressive skills, self-expression (5.4)*
>
> *Technical skills (4.0)*
>
> *Builds self-confidence (7.3)*
> *Develops whole person (7.4)*
> *Develops empathy (9.3)*

Effects claimed for drama were considerable and wide-ranging. A noticeable aspect of the nature of the responses for drama was that effects were perceived to be operating through a number of aspects of drama teaching – through content (issues-based themes), process (group work and discussions) and dramatic techniques (role and thought tracking). Overall, there tended to be an emphasis on effects related to the development of pupils as individuals, and their relationships with others.

Notably absent from claims for drama was the development of knowledge about cultural traditions, and multiculturalism. There were also minimal claims made for the development of creativity (although more for the related category of thinking and problem-solving skills).

Visual art

> *Fosters self-esteem (7.2)*
> *Transfer of knowledge and skills (12.3)*
>
> *Technical skills (4.0)*
>
> *Awareness of pupils' surroundings (2.2)*
> *Knowledge and understanding of the artform (1.1)*

Although, in common with drama and music, the development of self-esteem was endowed with considerable importance for visual art, art was also distinguishable by a focus on skills and knowledge of the artform itself.

There was not a focus, in claims from visual art teachers and other interviewees, on art developing communication skills and language. However, art was seen to provide opportunities for pupils to express themselves and develop expressive skills in a form not dependent on high levels of literacy. Specific categories related to social skills such as teamwork were also not often evident in claims for visual art.

Music

> *Technical skills (4.0)*
>
> *Fosters self-esteem (7.2)*
>
> *Teamwork (10.1)*
>
> *Knowledge and understanding of the artform (1.5)*
>
> *Fulfilment, enjoyment, pleasure (11.1)*

The development of technical skills and self-esteem were key effects for music. Music was also characterised by an emphasis on teamwork (performing and composing in groups) and on enjoyment. Like art, although music was seen as an artform where pupils could express themselves, claims were not made relating to the development of communication skills and language. Music was also absent in claims for increased awareness of surroundings and of social issues, and although some claims were made for the transfer of knowledge and skills from music to other curriculum areas, these claims were significantly lower than those made for visual art and drama.

English

> *Knowledge and understanding of the artform (1.4)*
>
> *Develops knowledge of cultural traditions (2.1)*
> *Develops creativity (6.2)*
>
> *Develops empathy (9.3)*
> *Transfer of knowledge and skills (12.3)*

English teachers, in contrast to music, art and drama, emphasised knowledge of the artform and of cultural traditions – as discussed earlier in the chapter, an aspect of this was a focus on broadening pupils' horizons through experiences in 'high culture' such as theatre trips. A focus on creative writing was evident in the developing creativity effect (6.2). Claims for the development of social skills and teamwork were notably absent from English.

Dance

> *Enhances physical health (11.3)*
>
> *Knowledge and understanding of the artform (1.2)*
>
> *Technical skills (4.0)*

A distinctive feature about the effects claimed by dance teachers was the focus on physical health and fitness.

CONCLUSION

The four most commonly perceived effects (fosters self-esteem, transfer of knowledge and skills, technical skills and development of expressive skills) were recognised, to varying extents in most of the artforms. In fact, of the 12 most cited specific effects, nine of them are evident across all artforms. However, alongside these common aspects, examining the typology of effects from the perspective of individual artforms illuminates some interesting variations. Differences in emphasis emerged, and teachers articulated different aims and outcomes for pupils as a result of their experiences in a particular form of art.

As proposed in Chapter 2, a challenge for this study is to attempt to substantiate the claimed effects discussed in this interim report – an interesting aspect of this could be to what extent differences in artform are still evident. Whatever the outcome of this, the differences in perceived effects for each artform discussed in this chapter suggest that further investigations (in this study and beyond) need to keep open the possibility of artform-specific differences. Pupil perceptions of effects of the arts – including differences by artform – are discussed in the following chapter.

4. PUPILS' PERCEPTIONS OF
THE EFFECTS OF ARTS EDUCATION

INTRODUCTION

Clearly, a principal method of attempting to corroborate teachers' accounts of the effects of arts education is to garner corresponding perceptions from pupils. As described in Chapter 1, one way this study is collecting the pupil perspective is through a longitudinal series of interviews with a small group of Year 7 and Year 9 pupils in the five secondary case-study schools. This chapter presents an initial and provisional analysis of these pupils' responses to the section of the interview that dealt with their perceptions of the outcomes of the arts education they had experienced. In order to allow the pupil voice to be represented in terms that are close and sympathetic to their own preferred vocabulary, the categories developed for the teacher typology (and presented in Chapter 2) have deliberately not been applied in the first stages of interpreting the pupil data.

As with the teachers' typology, the analysis of pupil responses also necessitates a considerable degree of fragmentation, which, at this stage in the research, results in a failure to capture the experience of the arts as a holistic phenomenon. In view of the longitudinal nature of the study, later analyses will attempt to rectify this problem by locating pupils' experiences in a broader biographical context.

WHAT IS ARTS EDUCATION FOR?

In the first open question from the schedule which sought to elicit pupil perspectives on their arts education, the general enquiry *'What is learning in the arts for at this school?'* was posed. Overall, responses here showed some clear differences between Year 7 and Year 9 pupils, but not particularly between the different artform enthusiasts. Though much less clear, there may also have been some slight variation in pupils' emphasis on 'creativity' as opposed to 'expression', depending on the nomenclature of the arts faculty ('Creative Arts' or 'Expressive Arts') in the different schools.

A number of different views were registered, and a rough ranking of the frequency of these is given overleaf. Particular emphasis was given to the expressive purpose of an arts education by the Year 9 sample, while others suggested its general educative broadening and enhancing nature. Personal and social development outcomes such as increased self-confidence, self-esteem and cooperation also featured with some regularity.

Year 9 sample: *What is learning in the arts for at this school?*	
• **self-expression** (thoughts and/or feelings)	*it's to express what you feel in different ways* *getting things inside you out* *expressing your thoughts* *expressing ideas and feelings*
• **general education enhancement**	*to give us more experience* *to learn things and find out new things* *it's part of our education ... broaden our mind* *to look at things differently*
• **confidence**	*giving you more confidence saying what you believe in* *confidence – it's opened me up* *gives confidence in how you do things* *self-esteem ... feeling you've achieved something*
• **creativity and imagination**	*learning how to use your imagination* *doing something more creative* *widen your imagination* *be creative*
• **artistic education**	*recognising how art is structured* *learning different artforms* *learning different skills*
• **career**	*if you like it, you can take it further, as a job*
• **future enhancement**	*it's something you carry with you forever* *something you might do in your spare time* *for education later in life*
• **social cooperation**	*working with others, listening to their ideas* *working together and getting involved*

A single respondent referred to empathy ('... *taking a different person's point of view*') and a small number emphasised different forms of therapeutic benefit ('*relaxing*', '*enjoyment*', '*an escape from normal life*'). Only one Year 9 pupil '*did not know*' any purpose for arts education. Overall, the personal and social dimension of the arts education figured highly in the Year 9 responses.

In contrast, about half a dozen Year 7 pupils said they did not know what doing arts in their school was for. Even more notable as a finding was the fact that, unlike their Year 9 counterparts, the highest-ranking response from Year 7 pupils in three of the five schools revolved around the view that the purpose of arts education was somehow related to career or job prospects (e.g. becoming an '*actor*', '*artist*', '*architect*', '*musician*', '*dancer*', etc.) Such instrumental interpretation of the purpose of an arts education from the younger age-range sample does raise interesting issues. Equally, the Year 7 sample frequently responded by defining the purpose of arts education somewhat literally as the acquisition of arts techniques and skills. After that, such outcomes as fun and enjoyment featured. Compared with the Year 9 sample, very much smaller numbers referred to the personal development aspects such as confidence, general education enhancement, self-expression, creativity and cooperation. Notwithstanding this, the calibre of responses by Year 7 pupils was in no way less articulate than their Year 9 peers, and indeed several made particular comments about the difference between arts and other subjects such as sciences or maths:

> *It helps you develop yourself a lot. I mean, say with biology, it doesn't actually go into how you feel and things, it's just 'Dissect this frog', basically.*

> *I think arts gives you a chance, because in maths you're just set to do this and you know you have to do it all the way through, but with art and drama you just kind of, you know, do it if you want to do it, and you do it your own way. Instead of 'Oh, you have to [multiply] this one' ... [in the arts] there's not an answer; it's doing it your own way.*

The rough rank order of Year 7 responses was as follows:

Year 7 sample: *What is learning in the arts for at this school?*	
• **career or job**	*they need to know about those sort of things when they have to get a job* *if you want a future career in the arts; if you want to be an actress, artist* *it helps you, like if you want to be an actor, when you grow up* *you've got a better way of getting a job if you can play instruments or draw*
• **artistic education**	*helps you learn the basic skills for art* *helps you gain knowledge and techniques* *to understand different things of the subject*
• **creativity**	*to have a creative mind* *to find out what creative skills you've got* *to learn what we didn't know before, creative things* *to find your potential of how creative you are*
• **enjoyment**	*enjoyment, and to really get something out of it* *it's enjoyable, everyone seems to like* [them]
• **confidence**	*being confident to say and do things straightaway* *not to be scared to express yourself*
• **general education enhancement**	*get you interested in different aspects of the world* *some kind of education* *appreciate some of the more beautiful things in life*
• **self-expression**	*to express your feelings, how you feel without writing it down* *to express your opinions and work with your own ideas* *to develop yourself, going into how you feel*
• **cooperation**	[it's for] *working well together* *make you cooperate*

A single Year 7 respondent noted the therapeutic aspect of arts ('... *if I'm angry or upset, I can sit down and play music and feel better'*), and how arts allowed everyone to achieve ('...*it's about getting achievement; everyone can get something out of it'*). One Year 7 girl indicated at this point she felt music had helped her coordination for ball games and also reading, and a Year 7 male respondent chose to state arts helped him present work neatly.

THE EFFECTS OF VISUAL ARTS EDUCATION

All pupils in the Year 7 and Year 9 samples were asked what they had learnt in the visual arts, and then the question '*What have been the effects on you of doing art?*' was posed. Again, some notable differences in the two age groups emerged.

The outcomes mentioned most by the Year 7 sample included enjoyment, and also particular references were made to a sense of improvement in their own artistic ability, with comparisons between the primary school visual art curriculum and their current opportunities and experiences in the subject much in evidence. Equally, pupils frequently compared their sense of having poor art skills at primary school with the burgeoning confidence and belief in their own ability accruing from the first year of key stage 3 art teaching. Others made reference to their changed visual awareness ('*looking differently*' at '*things*' or '*paintings and art work*') or to their enhanced understanding of artists, art and materials/media. Allied to this, some pupils chose to stress their sense of acquisition of new (or basic) art skills.

Much less often, Year 7 pupils mentioned outcomes in terms of self-expression, ('*saying how you feel*', '*how to express yourself*') and only two referred directly to a sense of satisfaction or achievement as an effect of their visual arts education. Just one pupil employed the term imagination.

Five Year 7 pupils felt unable to provide an account of any effects.

Put together, the tenor of responses from this sample of Year 7 pupils suggests that they were particularly aware of skill enhancement and collectively conveyed a strong sense of internal progress and proficiency both with the medium and with their capacity to appreciate and understand the visual world and art. At this stage of their visual art education, it was the outcomes of technical and visual empowerment rather more than personal growth which appeared to dominate their thinking. Indeed, one Year 7 pupil noted this precisely when she commented:

> '*cos I'm in the first year, I haven't learnt to draw my own views yet ... it probably will mean a way of expressing yourself, but at the moment I don't feel anything when I paint.*

Year 7 sample: *What have been the effects on you of doing visual art?*	
• **enjoyment**	*it's enjoyable, fun ... relaxing* *I enjoy art more, looking at paintings*
• **improvement in artistic ability**	*all I knew was how to draw, but now you can do really good skills with shading and rubbing it in* *it's stretched my ability of what I'm able to do, 'cos before in primary we just did painting and making cards* *it's made my art work better* *I am more used to painting and drawing; nowadays I would try and draw, I will have a go ... I'm more confident, I'm getting better at it*
• **changed visual awareness**	*it's made me a lot more aware of colours – it's made me look more closely at everything and in more detail* *I look at things differently than I did when I first came; it's broadened my horizons – you look more closely ... it brings you much more together and you can see everything in its place – you see the dark and the light shades and where the light is hitting it* *I can see things I wouldn't have seen otherwise*
• **enhanced understanding**	*it's helped me understand some other painters and the way they made things* *I'd know now how much went into a painting*
• **skill acquisition**	*they teach you the basics* *they teach you how to do things, rather than to just do things; they show you how to do it*
• **satisfaction**	*it's given me a tremendous amount of achievement and pleasure and satisfaction, just seeing my work in front of me ... thinking I can improve that ... I feel fulfilled*

In contrast to this, the Year 9 sample's responses focused much more on the personal dimension, with some aspect of self-expression, particularly of feelings, being the most frequently cited effect. Expansion of self, in terms of confidence and a sense of having ability also featured highly, while increased imagination also was referred to as a factor of this personal growth and self-esteem. Unlike the Year 7 pupils, the Year 9 sample usually did not just reference increase in artistic competence – skills, visual appreciation or understanding. Their responses also included accounts of satisfaction and achievement and growth. There were more examples of pupils suggesting visual art's relaxation value in the Year 9 sample.

Year 9 sample: *What have been the effects on you of doing visual art?*	
• **self-expression**	*how to express, it's a sense of freedom ... there's all these techniques and something else – it just gives you a sense of euphoria in a way being able to notice you've created this piece* *I suppose you can express yourself more by doing art, who you are, what type of things are interesting* *I've learnt how to express myself ... you can make it look like you feel* *it gives me a chance to express feelings and I don't have to do it verbally where you might get stuck – you want to say something but you don't want to*
• **expansion of self**	*it boosts my confidence, it really spread my ideas and learned me new skills so when I leave school I have lots of confidence to do things which I wouldn't do 'cos I was not confident enough ... it's all to do with confidence, finding the confidence that you have got the ideas, you can think them up and they are not silly* *it makes me feel I don't have to worry about what other people say, I can do just what I want, and show it how I want, be who I'd like to be through my art work – sometimes you can't be yourself 'cos of what people think and say; it's kind of a hidden message* *it's like realising stuff you didn't realise before – seeing things in a different light; if you don't actually look, you never experience it – and even if you're just looking, you're still keeping the images in your mind*
• **increased imagination**	*it can make you more imaginative – you think up your own ideas better ... and having your own ideas means you don't get bossed around, you don't have to listen to everyone else all the time* *it's given me different views – I feel more creative than when I first arrived, I feel more competent at expressing my views artistically* *I don't do anything NORMAL – I just put my imagination into it ...* *it gives you a good feeling inside yourself that you have this imagination inside yourself which can make you do all these things, draw things*

• **satisfaction/achievement**	*I like it and I'm good at it; when you do a good piece of work, you're satisfied with it. I just do it for my own satisfaction* *it's made me more able to do things, it gives me something I know I can do which is nice* *I'm good at it, it makes me look good in front of others. Since being new here and people thinking I'm not much good, to be able to look good in one subject is good – and that helps in other subjects*
• **relaxation**	*it's quite relaxing; you concentrate on what you're doing when you're painting so your mind is not on troubles* *I really enjoy art, it relaxes me. I think of it not as a subject I'd work in but something to relax me – just thinking about how to do this or that, or what we've learnt, it relaxes me. I could sit there for hours*

THE EFFECTS OF DRAMA EDUCATION

When the sample were asked their views on the effects of drama, a range of responses similarly emerged, but, in comparison with visual arts, there appeared to be some notable differences between schools, rather than just between age-groups. It is at least possible that this related to the fact that drama as a subject in its own right does not have national guidelines, and therefore the curriculum experienced by the pupils resulted in different emphases, e.g. on performance and theatre skills in two instances, as opposed to a strong focus on social realism/issue-based drama evident in one school. The outcomes from these different approaches and philosophies as described by pupils did show some diversity, particularly in the area of empathy/understanding of others: '*I understand now how other people feel and what they are like.*' Examples of this effect were very much less apparent in the accounts of pupils whose experiences had a more theatrical or performance orientation. However, this latter group exclusively referred to awareness of stagecraft or acting skills (e.g. '*it's made me a lot more appreciative of different actors*', '*understanding why actors do things and the sets*').

Some outcomes were outlined by the sample as a whole. An increase in confidence and the social or cooperative opportunities were the two major recurring effects mentioned by pupils from all five schools, though in each of these, a number of different aspects were actually being described.

Thus, when pupils spoke about their increased confidence, in some instances reference was actually being made to self-projection (e.g. '*speaking up in front of others*', '*I'm not scared now to get on stage*', '*I used to mumble*'), while others were actually indicating new capacities of self-expression ('*saying what you feel*', '*express what you are thinking ... talking out your ideas more*', '*I'm not afraid to ask the teachers or tell them what I think*'). Beyond that, some pupils' accounts of enhanced confidence in effect mentioned self-development: '*I've more personality now*', '*I've actually taken one girl out of another*', '*it's allowed me to open myself up more, make me more lively*', '*helps you be more imaginative ... if you don't imagine anything you're just like boring*'. Increase in self-awareness was also raised by a Year 9 respondent: '[Drama] *helps you understand yourself – how you feel and look, what you're doing or what you think.*'

In a similar way, differences and gradations in the accounts of social opportunities were evident. In some instances, pupils simply referred to the value of social interaction ('*it makes you talk to other people more*'), particularly with other than existing close friends. Others took this a step further and mentioned how in their view, drama allowed occasion for making new friends: '*helps you get together; there is a bond ... you make more friends*'. Beyond that, specific references to the capacity to develop social and cooperative skills were evident (e.g. '*learning about getting along together*', '*how to work in groups better*', '*how to work with others that you don't always get on with*' and '*group work is needed everywhere; I've got that skill now*'). More rarely, a Year 9 pupil inferred a level beyond cooperation, touching on the fact that drama's social processes – rather than content – could facilitate some sort of empathetic support: '*In drama, you've got to not think of yourself as yourself as such and think of the others – thinking and trying to help them get their ideas across.*'

The development of empathy and awareness of others was another nominated effect of drama. For some, this was articulated in terms of recognition of others' behaviour and attitudes (e.g. '*thinking about how another person thinks*', '*it gives you an awareness of how people behave*', and '*it gives you a chance to think about that thing from somebody else's point of view*'). Sometimes, feelings were given prominence (e.g. '*I understand how people feel*', '*you can understand better, if you've played that character or seen it, how they're feeling or what they're like*' and '*get insights into how they're feeling instead of how I'm feeling*'). Again, what might be seen as a higher level of response in this category came only from Year 9 pupils, and was a viewpoint that appeared to synthesise the awareness of others with personal growth:

> *By taking on the role of another person, you get to know how their lifestyle is and what it's like in real life ... it helped me understand how it felt at home ... drama helps you understand other people and helps you understand yourself as you get older.*

Other pupils (almost exclusively from one school which employed issue-based drama) mentioned outcomes reflecting new social awareness ('*we've learnt about serious issues*', '*you're more interested in real life, what's going on*') and, beyond that, something in the area of moral development (e.g. '*it taught me it's not nice to be* [racist] *and you've got to be nice to everybody individually ... it teaches you not to*', '*it teaches you what happens ... you know you shouldn't* [bully] *so you don't do it when you're older*' and '*you learn how you would react in a situation ... you also know that if something like that happened, you could react to it properly*').

Differences in the responses of the two age groups were not so immediately apparent in drama as in visual art. However, some gestation or refinement of ideas was evident in that it was pupils from the Year 9 sample who articulated most clearly the effects of drama on their own development, whether in terms of social skills, empathy or moral awareness.

THE EFFECTS OF MUSIC EDUCATION

The sample's response on the effects of their music education showed another form of variability. Replies in the area of music tended to show most marked differences amongst pupils at the same school and within the same class or year group, rather than as in art, suggesting developments in the views of the Year 7 and Year 9 sample, or distinct outcomes relating to different emphases within the curriculum as in drama. Thus, while many of the same features of the curriculum – composition, keyboard skills, rhythm, music appreciation, etc. – were described across the five schools, each school's sub-samples would express a wide range of viewpoints about the impact of these experiences. One factor here was the degree of musical knowledge and experience which pupils brought to their school music curriculum. Sometimes, those who were already proficient with an instrument suggested that the music learnt at school had no effect: '*It was all just things I'd done.*' In other instances, it was those pupils expressing the view that they had no musical ability who stated negative outcomes: '*it doesn't keep my interest, I don't enjoy it ... I don't know how to read music or anything, so that didn't really help*' and '*not an awful lot* [of effect] *really; I was never keen on music and if you're not keen, you don't learn as much*'.

A range of positive outcomes did emerge, though, and these came as much from musical experts and enthusiasts as from those who professed no expertise or specialist interest, and were evident in both the Year 7 and Year 9 samples. Overall, the issues of differentiation, curriculum relevance and manageability may be particularly apparent in music education.

Some pupils elected to mention technical skills (e.g. '*given me a sense of rhythm*', '*know the language ... like semitone*', '*how to play keyboards*'), but the most common outcome was undoubtedly the increased ability and interest in listening to music, and beyond that, to appreciate and understand it more. This sensitisation might relate to other cultures and periods of music (i.e. a broadening repertoire of appreciation: '*I like more different varieties of music than I did before*') or to their ability to extract more meaning from the music they heard ('*it made me like music a lot more, being able to listen and think of all the different parts that people are doing*'). Appreciating the complexity of music making and composing ('*I realise a lot of work goes into music*') also featured. Others implied that the ability to discriminate was a salient outcome (e.g. '*I appreciate music more, I can recognise good music*', '*I now understand different ways of playing music can be effective or not so effective*').

Other types of response for music education made strong reference to affective outcomes: the sheer enjoyment of music ('*it's fun*') – whether playing or listening. The excitement and the relaxing or therapeutic nature of music were noted. The confidence to perform in front of others was noted as an effect occasionally and, equally, a few pupils referred to the social aspects of working together in a group, being part of a band or meeting new people. A few references were made to the expressive potential of music: '*I learnt how to express myself*', '*it's another way of expressing yourself*'.

Other responses indicated the self-esteem and sense of identity enjoyed by those who were players within the context of their school: '*it makes me feel good, 'cos I can actually do something not everyone else can do*' and '*if you play an instrument, you know you can do something*'.

THE EFFECTS OF DANCE EDUCATION

Approximately half the sample offered comments about dance: according to the pupils in two of the five case-study schools, it was not included within their arts provision. Hence, the topic of dance education was discussed with a total of 33 young people (18 in Year 7 and 15 from Year 9). Even among those pupils in each of the three remaining case studies who were experiencing dance education, there were – unlike in other arts subjects – several unsolicited references to the limited opportunities proffered within their current curriculum:

> *We don't do much dance ... it's a small subject* (Year 9).

> *Well, over the last three terms, we have only done about six dance lessons* (Year 9).

> *Not much dance, we have only done a term on it* (Year 7).

> *We didn't have hardly any lessons* (Year 9).

A further feature of some pupils' responses was an indistinctiveness as to what dance actually was. Some of the depictions of what they had learnt in dance required reference to other subjects:

> *I consider it a modern day PE. It's just like using your body – the difference is with dance you are just making movements out of your body and you do little steps* (Year 7).

> *It is more or less like drama; it's more ideas* (Year 9).

> *It's an expressive thing, using your body – it doesn't have to be moving, it can be just a still picture, someone bending over, or someone lying on the floor with their leg up – I think that is the only art thing* [about dance] *which will have a little amount of effect – I'm not a great mover* (Year 9).

Clearly, this sense of a somewhat cursory engagement with a subject somewhat lacking in definition needs to be borne in mind and may be a contributory factor in the views and attitudes expressed during the interviews. Indeed, when asked directly about what had been the effects of dance education, it was noticeable that the most common response from about half (15) of the youngsters was that it had none (e.g. '*... not really anything*', '*nowt*' and '*it won't give me anything that's important*'). Notwithstanding this, a range of distinct responses about outcomes did emerge, as the pupils relayed what they had done in their dance lessons. As well as that, 18 youngsters, when asked, could affirm that their dance experiences did have some effects.

The most frequent pupil viewpoint on the learning outcomes of dance education referred to encountering and/or acquiring the fundamental elements of dance movement. Commonly, answers included the terminology of basics: '... *new steps*', '*the basic moves*', '*different movement*', '*use more than one dance routine*' and ' ... *the elements of dance*'. Sometimes, the accounts offered specific details: '*how to use our feet ... jump up and down*', '*now I can do cartwheels*', and '*I learnt just hand movements, body expressions ... stepping backwards and forwards*'.

An associated – but significantly different – perspective was offered by a number of other pupils, whose comments focused on enhanced body awareness outcomes accruing from engaging with the elements of dance. Typically, these responses made direct reference to learning about '... *using your body, what sort of movements I can make with my body*', '*it's told me what I can do with my body*', '*I've learnt about using my body to make a picture or express emotion*', '*... body expressions*'. A few pupils incorporated some aspect of connecting with musical elements in their answers: '*keep in time and dance different kinds of music*', '*doing things to a certain beat, listening to a rhythm*' and '*... you learn about keeping rhythm*'. While these variations may appear slight, it was noticeable that if 'encountering dance movement elements' was the only perceived learning outcome, the respondent was more likely to give a negative response when asked directly about the effects of their dance education. Those pupils who offered accounts suggesting an internalised or intrinsic impact of 'enhanced body awareness' and 'musical connection' usually had more positive comment.

One outcome that some of the sample associated with dance – and not expressed quite this starkly in relation to any other artform – was that it helped overcome shyness and embarrassment. The pupils – noticeably from one school in particular – saw dance as resolving anxiety about appearance:

> *People who didn't* [know about dance] *would've learnt not to be shy and that you won't make a fool of yourself – I think dance has taught me not to be ashamed of anything and be proud of everything I do ... because people don't do things because they think people will think they look stupid or something, and so dance can help you in lots of different ways* (Year 7).

> *When we first started dance, people just stood around and didn't want to do anything ... it's much better now 'cos everyone is not so shy and they just don't care what other people think, they do what they feel is good. That's good 'cos you don't want to be shy throughout your life* (Year 9).

> *I can dance really, nearly properly ... if you know how to dance, you can get up and dance rather than just sitting there. This is always better than just watching other people do it* (Year 9).

Offering confidence and self-belief, clearly closely linked to this defeat of deficit body image, was also mentioned in relation to dance:

You learn you can do it, it doesn't have to be big to be good — it makes me realise that you don't need so much power and strength; as long as you are responsible, you can achieve it (Year 9).

I got self-confidence, learnt lots of dance moves (Year 9).

Just doing it in front of the class, well that has made me more confident as well (Year 9).

It's made me different ... because I thought I was a bad dancer, like I couldn't dance and now I can (Year 7).

Other outcomes mentioned included a sense of freedom: ('[from doing dance] *you know you can do anything you want, you don't have to follow strict guidelines*') and creativity ('*... it has made you be more creative ... 'cos we've learnt to add little movements to make it more interesting*'). Relaxation also was suggested: '*... for some people it helps a lot because it helps relaxes and things like that*'. There were occasional references to social skills (e.g. '[helps with] *working in groups*'), and one or two pupils noted the benefits more in terms of the acquisition of useful social mores: '*It is always useful, I think, at balls; I know how to waltz*' and '*... I know I won't make a fool of myself when I go out clubbing*'. A couple of youngsters noted that encountering dance at school had begun further interest and commitment: '*I thought if I got into dancing at school, I might as well get into dancing actually in a* [dance] *club*' and '*... because I love dance so much, I have taken it more up as a hobby at home*'. Beyond leisure interest, a small number of pupils mentioned their sense of its value for future career aspirations: '*I want to be a choreographer, so it will help me a lot*' and '*... I would like to be a dancer; it has given me a lot of confidence*'.

Finally, rather than any aspect of personal enskilling or growth, a number of pupils chose to emphasise a new awareness of the boundaries of 'dance': '*it helps you see all aspects of dance, not just like on TV*' and '*I learnt that dance is actually about movement; I used to think it was just what the Spice Girls did*'. In one school, two pupils referred directly to the dance of other cultures:

We've been learning about different cultures and what [dances] *they do ... like with Red Indians ... we found out about their beliefs, and if they were having trouble, they would do special dances ... that's important 'cos you know not to hurt their feelings* (Year 7).

We've learnt different types of dance from different cultures. It showed me there wasn't just one type of dance like I used to think; there's many different types and they come from all over the world (Year 9).

Put together, pupil responses indicated that dance offered a wide range of effects. Within the arts, it clearly was felt to make a unique contribution to such outcomes as self-realisation and self-confidence, particularly in terms of body awareness. Equally, there was not a clear gender divide in the views about dance: some of the boys in the sample were very positive about their experiences, while a number of girls gave accounts which indicated minimal interest. There were boys and girls who commented on their inability to dance. A major issue is obviously the limited opportunity and location within the curriculum for dance to be effective in achieving its particular impact.

THE EFFECTS OF ENGLISH EDUCATION

A total of ten pupils (six from Year 9 and four from Year 7) discussed English as an artform. This small sub-sample actually came from three different schools, although the Year 7 youngsters and two of the Year 9 respondents were all from one school with a strong tradition in literature. Notwithstanding this, a common resonance did emerge across the responses: there was a distinct view from these pupils that English offered a medium, a manipulable raw material – i.e. words and style – by which they attained other outcomes such as self-expression or self-awareness. Thus, it was the activity of text creation – rather more than literature appreciation – which was particularly volunteered as an example of an 'other' arts subject. While this may reflect the place in the interview where English as 'other arts' was discussed (i.e. after art, drama, music and dance had been described in turn), it does also suggest that, for these pupils, learning in English was about being empowered to make literature, not just to receive it, and certainly was what gave it special value and arts status.

Examples of this control of the medium emerged in pupil responses to the question about what they had learnt:

> *I've learnt how to use language and different vocabulary – [writing poetry] sort of makes your mind flow ... you just find a word and try and use it somewhere ... it makes your mind really flow* (Year 7).

> *Lots of things like similes and adjectives and alliteration ... it's helped me with my poetry a lot 'cos I really like writing poetry, I'm quite good at it really ... it means being able to express yourself a lot* (Year 7).

> *I've learnt that you don't have to use plain sentences to express what you feel; you can compare things with everyday life to make it sound like you feel* (Year 9).

> *You can be creative, be somebody else and you can write paragraphs and paragraphs about what you are but then disguise it, write different poems and that ... there are lots of different ways of expressing the same sort of thing – you can make things sound happier or sadder than they are in real life* (Year 9).

Other outcomes did emerge from the pupils' accounts: sometimes respondents stated creativity as an effect ('*it brings out your creativity*') and self-expression was mentioned several times ('*how to express yourself, voice your opinions*' and '*... a chance to write what you are feeling*'). The cathartic effect of this ability to express feelings effectively was graphically illustrated in one interview:

English is important to me. It's probably because I'm quite good at it actually ... and that means being able to express yourself a lot. I've written quite a few things about my life – when I was about nine or ten, I was being quite bullied really. And I got very upset and quite depressed. And writing [about it] helped me get out of that. Because just reading that, I thought 'Well, it can't really be this bad'. It helped me to just make me feel more happy about myself. And just to be who I am. And if they don't like it, stuff them (Year 7).

A similar – if less intense – therapeutic effect was raised in another instance: '*You can use words to release some of the stressedness – or whatever the word is!*' Sometimes, the pupils spoke in terms of enhanced understanding or empathy (e.g. '*you deal with social issues*', '*you get a broader understanding of things*', '*... personally, I've learnt from writing poems that everything is not black and white*'), and one Year 9 boy linked the outcome of awareness of others with the interactive techniques used in his English lesson:

In English, you get to talk and discuss and put your views across – and you get lots of different people's views and you can see what other people think ... if we all listen to each other, then we know what each other's needs are and we can work around that.

Three of the pupils chose to include the wider 'literature appreciation' curriculum involved in discussing English as an artform, and mentioned the literature components: '*You learn that English isn't just a language. It's all the poetry, all the lectures and the reading, like literature and everything.*' However, one did declare:

For some lessons you have to use your imagination, to write stories and things, poems. They are the things I'm really good at. For studying text and things like that, that's a bit tedious – I have always read a lot (Year 9).

For one pupil only – a Year 9 girl – the development of literary appreciation was a perceived outcome:

I've been able to learn that when you read a story or a novel, it's not just the writing that's important, but it's the thought behind the writing, and I enjoy reading more now after learning more about the thoughts that authors have written about.

A final and recurrent theme in a number of these pupils' responses was the reference to the importance of English because of its significant career and learning currency. The high status of English within the curriculum was noted (e.g. '*it's one of the most important subjects ... English comes into all sorts of things*' and '*... it helps in other subjects, like science*'), as was its value in the world of work:

Writing is important because nearly every single job you have, you have to sort of write and if you don't use language that is sophisticated or anything, people just think you're not very clever or anything. So, it helps if you can use better language, like words and things (Year 7).

It was noteworthy that several of the pupils saw their own career path as intrinsically linked to their ability in English: in all, four directly mentioned the desire to be a writer or journalist:

> *I won a poetry competition recently ... I think I've changed a lot in English from primary school — my style of writing ... the way I write things is completely different ... I'd really like to do something on Radio 4, actually start as a journalist and work my way up. And English has sort of really helped me to, I don't know, see that that ambition might not be absolutely impossible ... so it's really important* (Year 7).

> *I would like to be a journalist, so English will affect me ... with different short stories and poems, you can learn to say what you want in a couple of lines. When you're doing stuff like that in English as a whole, you're learning stuff and you can use that to help you, it will always stay with me what I have learnt* (Year 9).

> *You can use English in other things ... you are only going to do art as a hobby or as an artist, as a career. I think I'd like to do something with literature — when you're writing reports, you've got to be grammatically correct, you need to know the correct way to put things, how to write things down* (Year 9).

It is worth noting again that these responses were from pupils who were well aware of English as an activity which involved manipulating language, style, form and so on. Equally, their sense of their own expertise shone through. Appreciation of English as an arts subject seemed directly related to, even dependent on, this sense of aptitude. As such, English's position within the canon of arts education may be distinctive: within current curriculum imperatives, could a perceived lack of verbal facility deter youngsters from even recognising, let alone engaging, with language as a creative medium?

CONCLUSION

The effects of arts education as pinpointed by the pupil sample overall proved extremely wide-ranging. Across the responses as a whole (i.e. leaving aside variations by school and artform), it was possible to see each of the 12 major categories of outcomes that were identified by the teacher sample, as outlined in Chapter 2. Overall, there was also a quite remarkable degree of consistency in the range of specific sub-category outcomes mentioned by pupils and teachers. Thus, apart from a small number of notable exceptions, the scope and nature of teachers' claimed effects received substantial corroboration from their pupils. There appeared to be only two key areas where the teachers' perceptions were not corroborated by the pupils:

- unlike teachers, pupils seldom articulated effects on their thinking skills and problem-solving processes (6.1);
- and, most significantly, the pupil sample offered few references to effects which transferred to other areas of the curriculum and learning (12.1-3).

The latter finding may suggest that teachers tend to underestimate the rigidity of pupils' compartmentalisation of school knowledge and, thereby, overestimate the extent to which their learning transcends subject boundaries. Alternatively, it may also indicate pupil mis-recognition of the transference of knowledge and skills – a possibility which raises an important methodological issue to which we return below.

In terms of the broad frequencies of testimonies to the effects of arts education, the pupil and teacher data are generally compatible. Certainly, teachers' emphasis on the outcomes associated with personal development and self-awareness received a ringing endorsement from the pupil sample. With the exception of the two areas noted above, pupils matched the high ranking teachers gave to such effects as technical skills, self-expression, knowledge of the artforms, team work, enjoyment/fulfilment and awareness of others.

Notwithstanding this, different artforms produced notable variation in perceived effects; and, significantly, in each of the arts subjects, certain categories of outcome did not emerge. In other words, no single artform appeared to provide the full canon of effects. Certain effects undoubtedly emerged only from examples of high-calibre teaching, but an overarching implication of the variability in outcomes between artforms clearly seems to suggest that a comprehensive arts education requires a contribution from all arts subjects.

Thus, the distinct differences between Year 7 and Year 9 responses about visual art produced evidence to suggest technical skills (Category 4) and knowledge, understanding and appreciation of the artform (Category 1) were very much the building blocks to achieve effects in the domain of thinking and creativity skills (Category 6), personal development (Category 7), intrinsic well-being (Category 11) and expressive skills (Category 5). Social skills, awareness of others or insights into the affective and social domain were notably lacking.

By contrast, in drama, not surprisingly, nominated effects appeared to cluster particularly around social skills (Category 10), awareness of others (Category 9) and also personal development (Category 7). Year 7 pupils were less likely to offer understanding of the affective domain (Category 3), again suggesting that arts effects are in some way linked to a maturation process. Appreciation of the artform (Category 1) also was rare in accounts of drama outcomes, and technical skills (Category 4) emerged only in the one school whose drama curriculum focused more on performance. Similarly, knowledge of the social domain (Category 2) was more evident in the school where drama teaching was very much issues- and process-oriented.

Frequently mentioned effects of music covered particularly knowledge, understanding and appreciation of the artform (Category 1), and, to a lesser extent, technical skills (Category 4), intrinsic well-being (Category 11), and personal development (Category 7). It thus showed commonalties with visual art, although thinking and creativity skills (Category 6) were not in any way so evident as in art. Knowledge of social and affective domains (Categories 2 and 3) was also largely absent.

Dance showed particular references to burgeoning technical and expressive skills (Categories 4 and 5) and self-awareness (Category 7). It again did not readily produce accounts of increased knowledge in the affective and social domain, social skills or awareness of others. Equally, appreciation of the artform was largely absent.

English as an arts subject appeared to produce most notable effects in the communication and expressive (Category 5) and creativity skills (Category 6) areas, as well as awareness of self (Category 7), and the social/affective domain (Categories 2 and 3); although, these were clearly related to pupils' sense of their technical skills (Category 4).

The results also demonstrated how all the artforms, though particularly music, appeared to have different effects on individual pupils, according, for example, to their various interests, aptitudes, needs and experiences. A further feature was the high incidence of references to extrinsic and instrumental purposes, particularly noted by younger pupils as an effect of their arts education generally. Although this study is almost exclusively concerned with arts education in the secondary phase, many of the Year 7 pupils' comments intensify concerns about the level of technical skills in the arts at the end of key stage 2 and about the poor quality of pupils' understanding of the purposes of the arts curriculum on entering key stage 3.

To conclude, it is appropriate to return to the chapter's central finding: namely, as to the salient outcomes of arts education in the secondary phase, there was much common ground between teachers' perceptions and those of their pupils – albeit pupils favourably disposed towards at least one of the artforms. Taken together, the two sources of data provide a credible testimony to the positive effects of some school-based arts on some children.

This evidence would be even more compelling if (a) teachers' and pupils' accounts could be verified or triangulated by the perceptions of others, (b) larger samples could be canvassed and (c) non-perceptual data in the form of so-called 'objective' measures of outcomes could be compiled. Subsequent stages of the project will include methods to address (a) through collecting the perceptions of employers, and possibly parents, and (b) through a survey of Year 11 pupils. The third option (c), while offering the tantalising prospect of progressing beyond perceptual evidence – which, is always susceptible to the charge of collective distortion or mis-recognition – poses severe methodological problems, especially in relation to the many complex and intangible characteristics surrounding the outcomes of arts education. For us, the two major difficulties centre on problems in achieving external validity of 'objective' measures of arts education outcomes and in garnering any evidence of causality between the arts inputs and the assessed outcomes. Notwithstanding these difficulties, an attempt to explore the possibilities of non-perceptual data as a source of understanding the effects of arts education was included in the initial phase of the study. As we shall see in the following chapter, it was the second of the methodological challenges – namely, interpreting the direction of causality – which turned out to be highly significant.

5. STUDYING ARTS-BASED SUBJECTS AND GCSE PERFORMANCE

INTRODUCTION

As described in Chapter 2, when invited to identify the effects of arts education, the teachers and senior managers interviewed in the five case-study secondary schools frequently mentioned the transference of knowledge and skills acquired in arts subjects to other areas of the curriculum. Teachers' references to this kind of a transfer effect were associated with all the artforms, though they were particularly related to visual art and drama, much less so to music. In sharp contrast, pupils seldom referred to any of the artforms having this form of transfer effect. In order to explore the prospects of finding some empirical signs of such a transfer effect, this chapter presents an analysis of the possible relationships between the taking of arts-based courses at key stage 4 and general performance in GCSE examinations. Unlike the previous three chapters, it entails an examination of non-perceptual data.

Searching for evidence of possible causal relationships between studying the arts and wider academic attainment has become something of a specialised genre within the research literature on arts education. Typically, research projects in this tradition examine the purported impact of taking arts courses on such outcome-related variables as general academic attainment, self-concept (including self-esteem), spatial ability, and, less frequently, locus of control, creative thinking and appreciation of the arts (e.g. Luftig, 1994). Most of this type of inquiry emanates from the USA (e.g. Du Pont, 1992; Forseth, 1980; Gardiner et al., 1996; Rauscher et al., 1997), though similar studies have been carried out in other countries, including, for example, Switzerland (Spychiger et al., 1995) and Hungary (Kokas, 1969). Very little such work has been conducted in the UK. Often focusing on the Kodaly method, music education is the predominant artform studied (Fox and Gardiner, 1997; Wolff, 1978). Much of the research adopts a quasi-experimental methodology and is generally informed by a psychological, if not psychometric, perspective. It tends to use primary or elementary school-aged pupils as its subjects. As a general rule, these studies investigate specific or additional arts-oriented teaching programmes, though data on the nature and mediation of these courses are often lacking. A recent review of studies in this field has been conducted by Sharp (1998).

The empirical evidence to support a possible association of wider learning outcomes with arts education would clearly bolster the case for the arts in the curriculum. Most probably, this reason alone constitutes a key motive for much of the funding for this field of inquiry. However, couched in this way, the approach leaves itself wide open to the criticism that it implicitly assumes that the direct effects of experiences in the arts are in themselves weak grounds to claim a significant place in the school timetable. Something of these concerns, for instance, were voiced by an audience of a recent example of this line of research (Fox and Gardiner, 1997):

> *The group were very cautious about placing too much emphasis on the consequential learning which can occur from music education, and wished to stress that the raison d'être for music was its own intrinsic value* (School Curriculum and Assessment Authority, 1997, p. 29).

Elliot Eisner (1998) makes a similar point more stridently: in a sceptical review of the American literature on research into the alleged impact of the arts on academic achievement, he observes:

> *We do the arts no service when we try to make their case by touting their contributions to other fields. When such contributions become priorities, the arts become handmaidens to ends that are not distinctively artistic and in the process undermine the value of art's unique contributions to the education of the young* (Eisner, 1998, p.15).

It was partly to recognise the force of such arguments that, when the RSA sought to launch a study which would include an investigation into the possible 'spin-off' or transfer effects of taking arts courses, it did so by setting this particular area of inquiry in the context of a wider-ranging programme of interrelated research that would examine all the outcomes of arts education – direct and indirect alike. It is hoped that the evidence and analyses initiated in the previous chapters have demonstrated the study's commitment to this comprehensive approach. Furthermore, it is important to stress that this initial and exploratory step into the analysis of some evidence on the possible relationship between the taking of arts courses at key stage 4 and general GCSE academic attainment should not be seen as an isolated enterprise, but as an integral and unfolding part of a much broader research agenda. For this particular aspect of the research programme, it made sense to begin by exploring the issues through an analysis of some existing data.

SECONDARY DATA ANALYSIS

Qualitative claims about effects which transfer from the taking of arts courses to other areas of the curriculum have included the proposition that experiences in the arts can raise general academic attainment in 16+ examinations. In view of this, and the increased availability of data for 'value-added' type analyses of performance at 16, possible links between GCSE achievement and the taking of key stage 4 arts-oriented courses seemed an appropriate area to start an examination of the claims for a transfer effect.

Consequently, in order to study the possible relationships between studying arts-related GCSE subjects and overall performance at GCSE, some secondary analysis has been carried out on data collected for the NFER's QUASE ('Quantitative Analysis for Self-Evaluation') service to secondary schools. The QUASE service provides information to schools about their own performance, relative to what might be expected given their pupils' prior attainment and their social context. The rich database of information collected about the schools and their GCSE pupils enables investigators to determine the relationships between GCSE results, other outcomes, and a range of background variables at the level of both pupils and schools. For current purposes, the investigation focused on the possible effects of taking key stage 4 arts-related courses on general performance in the GCSE examinations.

The three arts-related subject areas whose impact was to be studied were art, drama and music. QUASE data from a total of 152 schools with up to three cohorts of Year

11 pupils taking GCSEs between 1994 and 1996 were analysed; the total number of pupils in the sample involved in the analysis was 27,607. The sample of schools included cases of all the main types (e.g. co-educational, single-sex, inner city, rural, selective, independent), and analyses of the QUASE schools showed that they were broadly similar to the national distribution in terms of type of school, type of LEA, region and GCSE performance (Schagen, 1996).

The possible influence of studying the above subjects was investigated using multilevel modelling, controlling for most of the school and pupil level background variables which are known to be related to GCSE performance, including measures of prior attainment at around Year 7. Other background variables controlled for included, *inter alia,* gender, age, ethnicity, free school meal entitlement, ESL, SEN status, average attendance of individual pupils, type of catchment area and percentage of pupils in each school entitled to free school meals.

SETTING UP MULTILEVEL MODELS

In addition to the standard QUASE variables related to sex, age, ethnicity, prior attainment, etc., some new indicators were developed for pupils who had studied the three selected arts-related subjects.

ART	takes the value 1 if the pupil has entered at least one GCSE in the subject area of art, 0 otherwise;
DRAMA	takes the value 1 if the pupil has entered at least one GCSE in the subject area of drama, 0 otherwise;
MUSIC	takes the value 1 if the pupil has entered at least one GCSE in the subject area of music, 0 otherwise.

Some care had to be taken, however, in including these variables as they stand in the multilevel model. There are a significant number of pupils in the model with no GCSEs at all, as well as many with just one or two. Each of the above indicators is more likely to be positive for pupils taking a non-zero number of GCSEs, and therefore their effect is likely to be confounded with the overall effect of just taking one or more GCSE. To get round this, the analysis was carried out on a subset of pupils who had attempted three or more GCSEs.

As well as studying possible direct relationships between studying each of these subjects and GCSE performance, the opportunity was taken to investigate two other aspects of these relationships: 'interactions' and 'random slopes'. An interaction between studying a subject (say art) and another background variable (say sex) would imply that the relationship between art and GCSE performance was different for males and females. As well as considering possible sex interactions, the study also looked at interactions with prior attainment, so that hypothetically pupils with lower initial attainment might do more or less well if they studied one of the arts-based subjects.

Such interaction terms were included in the multilevel analysis by defining extra 'interaction variables':

ARTSEX	Interaction between studying art and gender
DRAMSEX	Interaction between studying drama and gender
MUSSEX	Interaction between studying music and gender
ARTXINT	Interaction between studying art and prior attainment
DRAMXINT	Interaction between studying drama and prior attainment
MUSXINT	Interaction between studying music and prior attainment.

The concept of 'random slopes' is based on the idea that the relationship between studying an arts-based subject and GCSE performance may not be the same across all schools, but may vary from school to school. The size of the school-level variance gives us an indication of the extent to which any 'arts-based subject effect' is consistent from school to school.

One further variable was developed, which was intended to represent the overall tendency of pupils to take arts-related subjects:

| ARTSPC | is the sum of the above three indicators, as a percentage of the total number of GCSEs attempted, e.g. an ARTSPC score of 25 per cent could mean that a pupil took four GCSEs, one of which was arts-related (say, music) or eight GCSEs, two of which were arts-related (say, music and drama). |

The multilevel analysis was carried out on the following measures of GCSE performance:

ENG	Average English score
MATHS	Average maths score
SCI	Total science score
AVREST	Average score on non-arts subjects.

It is considered that, in the context of the present inquiry, these variables represent the most appropriate indicators of general academic performance at GCSE. None of the other possible performance indicators which sum or average over all subjects was suitable, as they would include the arts subjects themselves.

RESULTS OF MULTILEVEL ANALYSIS

The multilevel analysis of QUASE data was carried out with three levels in the model: school, cohort and pupil. Background variables at the school and pupil levels were included, including prior attainment at or near intake to secondary school (e.g. on the basis of various verbal reasoning, non-verbal reasoning, English and maths tests). Once these basic models had been set up, the three arts-related variables and the six interaction terms were included. The variable ARTSPC, which measured the overall proportion of GCSEs which were arts-related, was included at a later stage.

To show the results of these analyses, the coefficients which express the estimated relationships between each of the arts-related variables (e.g. ART), the variables indicating GCSE performance (e.g. English GCSE results) and each of the background variables have been converted into 'effect sizes'. These may be regarded as equivalent to the correlation between the two variables when other variables in the model are taken into account. They represent the 'strength' of each relationship as a percentage, and allow the different variables to be compared in terms of their apparent influence on the test outcomes (e.g. SCI, AVREST), when all other variables are simultaneously taken into account.

Figures 5.1 to 5.4 show these effect sizes for each of the four outcome measures. For each variable, the estimated effect size is plotted as a diamond, with a vertical line indicating the 95 per cent confidence interval for the estimate. Any variable whose line intersects the horizontal zero axis can be regarded as not statistically significant (at the five per cent level). Positive values imply a positive relationship with the test score outcome; negative values imply that the test score tended to decrease with higher values of the given background variable.

For each of the three sex-related 'interaction variables' (e.g. DRAMSEX), positive values indicate a female bias, while negative values a male bias. Similarly, for each of the three prior attainment-related 'interaction variables' (e.g. DRAMXINT), positive values signal a stronger association for those with higher levels of prior attainment, while negative values signal a stronger association for those with lower levels of prior attainment. Interaction variables which were found to be clearly insignificant have been omitted from the figures (e.g. MUSSEX has been left out of Figure 5.1).

Figure 5.1   Effect sizes of arts-related variables on average English score

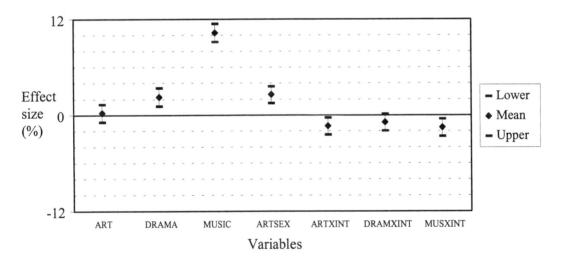

Turning first to Figure 5.1, which shows the relationships between the individual arts-related subjects and the English GCSE score, it appears that taking drama or music is significantly related to success in English. The estimated association between taking music and high attainment in English is particularly strong. Looking at interactions, art is the only subject to have a significant result for ARTSEX, and the result implies that the apparent effect of studying art is more positive for girls than for boys. Interactions with prior attainment show a stronger positive effect for art and music on those with lower levels of prior attainment.

Figure 5.2   Effect sizes of arts-related variables on average maths score

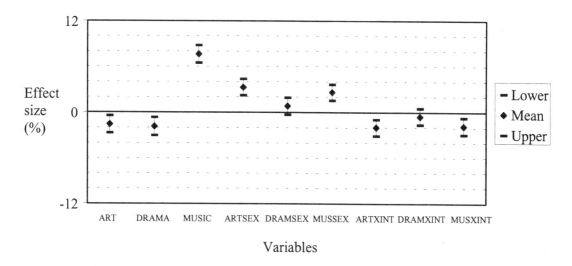

Looking at Figure 5.2, which shows the relationships between the individual arts-related subjects and the maths GCSE score, we can see that music again, as tradition would have it, is positively related to mathematics. However, the figure also indicates that there is a negative effect for art and drama: taking these subjects is associated with lower attainment in maths. Art and music are more positively associated with higher scores in maths for girls than for boys, for whom there is a corresponding negative association. Both these subjects have a stronger positive relationship with their average maths score for pupils of lower prior attainment.

Figure 5.3   Effect sizes of arts-related variables on total science score

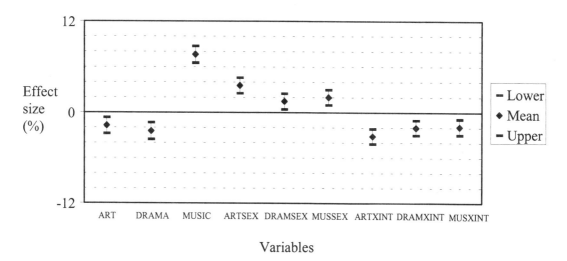

Figure 5.3, which shows the relationships between the individual arts-related subjects and the total science GCSE score, shows a similar picture to Figure 5.2. Music is positively associated with higher attainment in science, while art and drama are negatively related to science. All three arts-related subjects are more strongly

positively related to doing well in science for girls and for those of lower prior attainment.

Figure 5.4   Effect sizes of arts-related variables on average score for other subjects

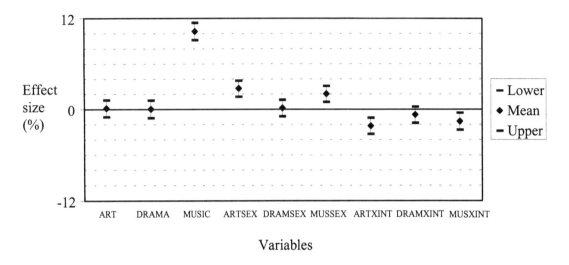

Figure 5.4 shows the relationships between the taking of arts-related subjects and the average score on non-arts subjects. A similar picture to the others is evident. Only music has a significant positive effect overall, while the other two subjects are not significant. Once again, art and music are more positively associated with higher average scores for all non-arts GCSE subjects for girls than for boys, and both have a stronger positive effect for pupils of lower prior attainment.

When we include, as a background variable, the percentage of arts-based subjects pupils took as a proportion of their total number of GCSEs, ARTSPC, there is a dramatic change. This is illustrated in Figure 5.5 for English, but it carried over into the analyses for all the outcome variables. The apparent effects of the individual subjects become much stronger and, for this analysis, art has a slightly stronger effect than music. These positive results, however, are counterbalanced by an even stronger negative effect of ARTSPC. What does this mean? One possibility is that each arts subject by itself may have some beneficial impact on performance in core subjects, but that pupils who tend to concentrate on arts subjects to the exclusion of others may have reduced academic attainment. None of the analysis carried out here gives any indications of causality, of course.

Figure 5.5   Effect sizes controlling for ARTSPC on average English score

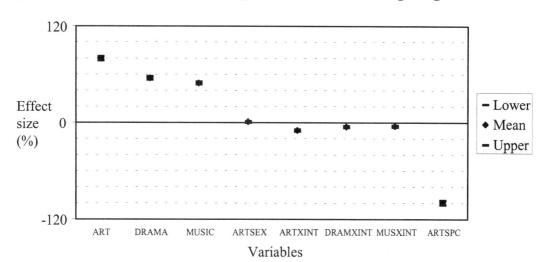

As mentioned earlier, the extent to which these relationships vary from school to school was investigated by making the coefficients for the three variables ART, DRAMA and MUSIC random at the school level. In all cases, this random effect was statistically significant, even when the overall relationship (e.g. between ART and ENG in Figure 5.1) was not apparently significant. The implication is that the impact of studying these subjects on pupils' performance is affected by one or more school-level factors. This suggests that in certain schools there are strong positive relationships between arts-based subjects and GCSE performance, while in others they may be non-existent or even negative. Table 5.1 shows the standard deviation between schools in the apparent change in GCSE performance associated with each arts-based subject.

Table 5.1   Standard deviations in slopes between different schools for GCSE results versus arts-based subjects

	ART	DRAMA	MUSIC
Average english score	0.31	0.45	0.40
Average maths score	0.33	0.45	0.67
Total science score	0.88	1.08	0.95
Average score for others	0.34	0.43	0.37

For practical purposes, the results for the total science score should be halved to account for the effect of double awards for integrated science.

DISCUSSION

When considering the meaning of these results, it is crucial not to lose sight of the fact that the analysis cannot offer any evidence of causality, or even the direction of causality. It is limited to highlighting associations between variables, which in the multilevel modelling technique deployed here are expressed as 'effect sizes', though this does not literally signify evidence of an actual 'effect'. For example, even if there is a positive association between x and y, it does not necessarily mean that x is causing y; it could also indicate that y is causing x, or that some other variable not fully controlled for is causing the association between x and y.

However, so long as these cautions about causality are respected, a number of possible and hypothetical explanations of the findings can be speculated upon, especially as a means of generating further lines of inquiry for other phases in the research programme. These hypotheses may be grouped under two main types or directions of causality:

(i)   the impact of studying arts-based subjects on general GCSE performance;

(ii)   the 'backwash' effect of predicted general GCSE performance on the take-up of arts-based courses.

Each of these possibilities is discussed in turn below.

The impact of studying arts-based subjects on general GCSE performance

In so far as they have produced some significant positive associations of the required type, the results of the analysis certainly do not rule out the possibility that taking certain arts-based subjects can have a beneficial effect on general attainment in GCSE examinations. That music in particular can have a positive transferable impact on GCSE performance in the core subjects is undoubtedly one possible and plausible interpretation of the results. Teacher accounts from the early fieldwork for the case study element of the research suggested that arts-related subjects could mediate such an effect through two main avenues: firstly, through increasing pupils' self-esteem and positive values towards school and learning (see Category 12.1/2 in Chapter 2) and/or, secondly, through developing transferable skills and knowledge (Category 12.3).

Proponents for the first of these avenues could argue that the findings are consistent with the view that, for some pupils, studying music is a highly positive and rewarding experience which nurtures a generalised and improved self-esteem and motivation and which in turn affects learning and performance in English, maths, science and other subjects. Thus, according to this proposition, taking music encourages a set of transferable values and attitudes that place a premium on the sense of personal fulfilment that can be achieved through learning. All the figures presented above show interaction 'effect sizes' consistent with the view that this form of effect through music may be particularly significant for pupils with lower levels of prior attainment.

Notwithstanding the above, a major difficulty for the positive values and self-esteem interpretation is that the results do not consistently display a similar effect for art and drama, contrary to teachers' testimonies from the case study evidence. If anything, more claims for generalised self-esteem were made for art than music, yet this is not borne out by the QUASE results. Art and drama (see Figure 5.4), for example, were found to have no significant association with pupils' general performance at GCSE as represented by their average score in non-arts subjects (AVREST). Even more problematically, art and drama were negatively associated with performance in maths (see Figure 5.2) and science (see Figure 5.3). This may suggest that art and drama do not generate the same transferable motivation towards learning as that alleged for music or, if they do, they also encourage a demotivating effect on learning in maths and science.

Very similar interpretations of the results could be mounted for the second broad type of mediating influence referred to above, namely, the claim that arts-related subjects develop transferable knowledge and skills (Category 12.3). From this perspective, it could be argued that the data lend support to the view that studying music leads to the acquisition of certain skills and knowledge which are relevant and helpful to pupils' performance in English, maths, science and other subjects. To some extent, this interpretation is in line with previous studies that have postulated a link between music education and the development of numeracy-related concepts (e.g. Fox and Gardiner, 1997). It is harder for this hypothesis to explain, though, why the 'effect size' for music on English (see Figure 5.1) is greater than that on maths and science (see Figures 5.2 and 5.3 respectively). Moreover, the proposition also lacks plausibility in accounting for the limited, or even negative, impact of art and drama on the test outcomes. It may be that the transferable knowledge and skills thesis is limited to music, but in the case study data, teachers saw it as much more likely to be associated with art and drama than with music.

The finding that taking a higher proportion of arts-related subjects is associated with reduced GCSE attainment (see Figure 5.5) poses substantial problems for both the transferable skills and the transferable motivation hypotheses, in so far as they relate to arts subjects as a collective entity rather than individual subjects. If either of these were tenable for the 'arts', it could have been expected that the greater the number of arts subjects taken by a pupil, the greater the transferability effects. The data suggest that the reverse is the case.

Both hypotheses could account for the variation from school to school as largely due to differences in the extent to which arts subject teaching accentuates positive experiences, self-esteem and/or transferable knowledge and skills. This underlines the need to study the processes of teaching and learning in the arts in order to avoid 'black box' approaches to input-output analyses.

The 'backwash' effect of predicted general GCSE performance on the take-up of arts-based courses

Many of the results generated by the QUASE analysis could be explained (hypothetically) by reversing the direction of causality implied in the propositions mooted above. Thus, rather than seeing the findings as an indication of the impact of taking arts-related subjects on GCSE attainment, they may be signalling the effect of predicted GCSE performance on the take-up of arts subjects in the light of pupils' academic attainment and experiences during key stage 3 (i.e. after the prior attainment assessments were taken).

According to this view, the results may be interpreted as showing that those pupils who had performed well academically throughout key stage 3 (allowing for both over-

and under-performers as measured by the prior attainment on intake), and were predicted to score highly in, say English (see Figure 5.1 and 5.2), were significantly more likely to take music (especially, if they are female) and slightly more likely to take drama than other pupils – though not so with art. Those doing well in maths (see Figure 5.2) were more likely to take music, but less likely to opt for art and drama; similar interpretations apply to science (see Figure 5.3) and general academic attainment, as indicated by the average score for non-arts subjects, but here there is no significant biased recruitment of high or low academic performers at key stage 3 for art and drama, though music attracts more high performers (see Figure 5.4). Why music rather than other arts-related subjects should recruit in this way may relate to the traditional perception of music carrying greater academic credibility and currency.

This line of argument also offers a very plausible explanation of the main feature of Figure 5.5, namely, that pupils who take a relatively higher proportion of arts-related subjects have reduced attainment at GCSE. According to the reverse effect thesis, this analysis reflects the tendency in many schools for only those pupils who are predicted to perform poorly at GCSE to be advised or allowed to include more than one arts subject in their GCSE portfolio.

Likewise, this set of hypotheses would probably account for the variation from school to school as being heavily influenced by the limitations and opportunities in the options structures of different schools. In this regard, the analysis may have unintentionally highlighted a set of issues that deserves further investigation. Do schools' options systems permit pupils to take more than one artform? What subjects are arts-based options usually set against? What factors, pressures and previous experiences influence pupils' choices regarding GCSE arts-based courses (e.g. whether to take a particular artform, whether to take more than one artform, or whether, as is often the case, to drop the arts altogether)? As a result of the implicit messages about the relative status of the arts contained in key stage 4 curricular structures, such questions have significant implications for both key stages in the secondary phase.

CONCLUSION

On balance, and with special regard to the arts as a whole, the explanation that best fits the overall thrust of the results is probably the second hypothesis, namely that the observed associations between general GCSE attainment and studying arts course at key stage 4 reflect qualities of the pupils who take-up the arts-related courses. In particular, this explanation provides for a plausible interpretation of the results for art and drama, as well as the negative effects associated with those pupils who take a high proportion of arts-related GCSE courses.

Music is a possible exception to this interpretation. Although the second hypothesis could provide a plausible account of the results for music, so could the first. Therefore, that this subject can impart a positive transferable impact on GCSE performance in the core subjects remains a possibility in the light of the analysis, although, even for music, problems with the transferable effect hypothesis surfaced in the results: anomalies were evident (e.g. the stronger association with English rather than mathematics) and in the case study research, teachers were more likely to attribute transferable effects to the other arts subjects than to music.

These interpretations are very tentative and reflect the complex nature of the results. It is conceivable, for example, that, given there are signs of multiple (sometimes conflicting) effects, the associations generated by the analysis could be caused by both hypothetical explanations impacting simultaneously, but in opposite directions of causality. Hence, the general thrust of the results to emerge from this part of the research lends support to those who have argued the case for caution when considering the claims made for transfer effects. Clearly, there is a need for further research in this field and this initial analysis of existing data serves to highlight the case for examining the impact of school-level factors on the relationship between taking arts-related subjects and general GCSE attainment . Furthermore, the results – particularly with regard to the negative associations of those taking high proportions of arts-related GCSEs – underline the value of Eisner's scepticism about the search for transferable effects at the risk of devaluing the direct outcomes and benefits of arts experiences at school. It is in that context that any further work on purported transferable effects should be firmly located. Certainly, it would be regrettable if the breadth and potency of teachers' perceptions of the outcomes of arts education (as illustrated in Chapters 2 and 3) – the majority of which seem to be verifiable from the pupil perspective (see Chapter 4) – should be undermined by elusive but attention-grabbing searches for evidence of extravagant claims about transfer effects to other areas of learning.

6. SUMMARY AND CONCLUSION

INTRODUCTION
This report has described the project's early work on the effects of arts education in secondary schools. In so doing, it has started to address the first of the study's four aims: (i) to document and evidence the range of effects and outcomes attributable to school-based arts education.

To this end, the report has drawn on detailed evidence collected through interviews with staff and pupils in five secondary case-study schools with a reputation for good arts practice. It has also used 'value-added' data on large groups of school leavers collected through the NFER's QUASE service.

TEACHERS' PERCEPTIONS OF EFFECTS
Chapter 2 identified and illustrated the perceived effects of school-based arts education, as seen by 48 teachers in the five case-study schools. An overview of these effects is set out below.

A. Effects on pupils:

1. Knowledge and appreciation of artforms/arts *(critical study & interpretive skills, historical contexts)*	2. Knowledge and understanding of the social and cultural domain *(traditions, social issues)*	3. Knowledge and understanding of the affective domain *(emotions, spirituality)*
4. Technical skills in the artforms/ arts *(tone, texture, movement skills, improvisation)*	5. Communication and expressive skills *(language, critical listening, self-expression)*	6. Thinking and creativity skills *(problem-solving, reflection, imagination)*
7. Personal development and self awareness *(understanding self, self-esteem, self-confidence)*	8. Personal skills *(sense of responsibility, organisational skills, autonomy, independence)*	9. Awareness of others *(tolerance, sensitivity, empathy, valuing of others and their work)*
10. Social skills *(teamwork, negotiation, life skills, cooperation, forming better relationships)*	11. Intrinsic: well-being effects *(enjoyment, pleasure, fulfilment, therapeutic outcomes, physical confidence)*	12. Extrinsic: transfer effects *(transfers to other areas of learning, employment, leisure involvement)*

B. **Effects on the school**: school ethos, pastoral system, behaviour management, school image.

C. **Effects on the local community**: impact on parents, governors and the local community.

D. **Art itself an outcome.**

Effects relating to pupils' 'personal development and self-awareness' (Category 7), especially the fostering of self-esteem, self-confidence and developing the whole person, received substantially more references from teachers than any other broad category of outcomes. For example, personal development outcomes attracted more nominations than all the direct artform knowledge and technical skills effects (Categories 1 and 4) put together. The second most frequently cited specific category referred to the perceived capacity of the arts to facilitate improvements in performance in other areas of the curriculum through the transference of skills and knowledge acquired in the arts (Category 12.3).

The effects volunteered by teachers were broader than the aims for arts subjects codified in the current National Curriculum. The breadth of the outcomes model and some evident commonalities in effects across different artforms suggest that there could be merit in including an overarching exposition of teachers' aims and aspirations for 'the arts' in a revised National Curriculum.

The scope and configuration of perceived outcomes associated with each artform varied substantially from one school to another. Most schools offered a broad vision in certain artforms and a narrower focus in others. It appeared that, to varying extents in each of the artforms, different schools or individual teachers were attempting to achieve different outcomes in their teaching of what is assumed to be the same 'subject'. This has important implications for any consideration of teacher effectiveness in the arts and suggests that a teacher's breadth of vision regarding the possible outcomes associated with a particular arts subject may itself be an essential characteristic of good practice.

VARIATIONS BY ARTFORM

Further analysis of teachers' perceptions of the outcomes highlighted the relative strengths and weaknesses of different arts subjects.

Although the encouragement of self-esteem was endowed with considerable importance for **visual art**, it was also distinguishable by a focus on technical skills and knowledge of the artform itself, as well as extending awareness of pupils' surroundings. Specific categories related to social skills, communication and language were not often evident in claims for visual art.

A distinctive feature about the effects claimed for **dance** was the focus on physical well-being and fitness. There was little mention of the development of critical skills or the making of aesthetic judgements about dance similar to those, for example, associated with the visual arts. This was felt to reflect its curriculum location within PE rather than within any 'arts' framework.

Effects claimed for **drama** were substantial and wide-ranging. Overall, there tended to be an emphasis on effects related to the development of pupils as individuals, and their relationships with others. Notably absent from claims for drama were the enrichment of knowledge about cultural traditions and the development of creativity.

The development of technical skills and self-esteem were key effects for **music**. Music was also characterised by an emphasis on teamwork and on enjoyment. Claims were not made relating to the development of communication skills and language. Music was also absent in claims for increased awareness of surroundings and of social issues.

English teachers, in contrast to music, art and drama, emphasised knowledge of the artform and of cultural traditions. A focus on creative writing was evident in the developing creativity effect. Claims for the development of social skills and teamwork were notably absent from English.

Contrary to what is generally held to be the case in the controversial debate about so-called transfer, 'spin-off' or 'Mozart effects', the research found that, although some claims were made for the transfer of knowledge and skills from music to other curriculum areas, the claims for this subject were substantially lower than those made for visual art and drama.

PUPILS' PERCEPTIONS OF EFFECTS

As providers of arts education, teachers' testimonies to its effects are obviously subject to some degree of natural self-interest. In recognition of this, the research was designed to collect accounts of the effects and effectiveness of arts provision from other constituencies, principal among which were the pupils. An analysis of pupils' perceptions of effects was included in the Phase 1 Report. It was based on interviews with 80 pupils (40 Year 7 and 40 Year 9 pupils).

What is learning in the arts for at this school? Pupils' responses to this question showed some clear differences between Year 7 and Year 9. Particular emphasis was given to expressive purposes by the Year 9 sample, though personal and social development outcomes such as confidence, self-esteem and cooperation also featured with some regularity. In contrast, very much smaller numbers of Year 7 pupils referred to personal development effects. Instead, they concentrated on career relevance and the acquisition of techniques and skills. These frequent references to narrow extrinsic and instrumental purposes of arts education may give rise to concerns about the quality of pupils' understanding of the aims of the arts curriculum on entering key stage 3.

Art (visual art). The tenor of responses from Year 7 pupils suggested that they were particularly aware of skill enhancement and collectively conveyed a strong sense of internal progress both with the medium and with their capacity to appreciate the visual world and art. In contrast, the Year 9 responses focused much more on the personal dimension, with some aspect of self-expression, particularly of feelings, being the most frequently mentioned effect. Expansion of self and a sense of visual art's relaxation value also featured highly.

Dance. Due to limited provision, under half of the sample were able to comment on the effects of dance. Although small in number, responses indicated that dance offered a wide range of effects, including making a unique contribution to self-realisation/ confidence outcomes, particularly in terms of body awareness. The major issue, however, was the limited opportunity within the curriculum for dance to be effective in achieving its particular impact as an artform.

Drama. A range of responses on effects emerged, but, in comparison with visual arts, there appeared to be some notable differences between schools, rather than just between age-groups. Perhaps reflecting its marginal status in the National Curriculum, the drama experienced by pupils resulted in different emphases, e.g. on performance and theatre skills in two instances, as opposed to a strong focus on social realism/issue-based drama evident in one school.

Music. Responses for music showed another form of variability: marked differences were apparent amongst pupils at the same school and within the same class or year group. Thus, while many of the same effects – technical skills, music appreciation – were described across the five schools, each school's sub-samples expressed a wide range of viewpoints about their impact. One factor here was the degree of musical knowledge which pupils brought with them.

The effects of arts education as pinpointed by pupils proved extremely wide ranging. Across the responses as a whole, it was possible to see each of the 12 major types of outcome identified by the teacher sample. Furthermore, teachers' emphasis on the outcomes associated with personal development and self-awareness received a ringing endorsement from the pupil sample. Overall, the scope and nature of teachers' claimed effects received substantial corroboration from their pupils, apart from two notable exceptions, which were rarely mentioned by pupils: thinking skills and transfer effects to other areas of the curriculum. The absence of pupil references to this latter outcome represents another important piece in the emerging picture of transfer effects.

Different artforms produced notable variation in perceived effects; and, significantly, in each of the arts subjects, certain categories of outcome did not emerge. Consequently, both the teacher and pupil data suggest that no single artform appeared to provide the full canon of effects. An overarching implication may be that a comprehensive arts education requires a contribution from all arts subjects.

Signalling the need for effective differentiation strategies, the results also demonstrated how all the artforms, though particularly music, appeared to have different effects on individual pupils, according, for example, to their various interests, aptitudes, needs and experiences. It was concluded that, taken together, the teacher and pupil data provide a credible testimony to the positive effects of some school-based arts on some children.

IS THERE A TRANSFER EFFECT FROM STUDYING ARTS-BASED SUBJECTS TO GENERAL GCSE PERFORMANCE?

As an alternative method of examining one of the claimed effects made by some teachers, the research also included a statistical analysis of quantitative data. This offered the advantage of complementing the study of effects through participants' perceptions of them with evidence that was essentially non-perceptual. This focused on the highly publicised claims regarding transfer effects (a sub-category in Category 12 in the teachers' outcome model), in particular that the taking of arts-based courses has a beneficial impact on a pupil's general academic performance at GCSE. The investigation focused on the possible effects of taking GCSE courses in art, music or drama on general academic performance in the GCSE examinations. NFER's QUASE data from a total of 152 schools with up to three cohorts of Year 11 pupils taking GCSEs between 1994 and 1996 were analysed; the total number of pupils in the sample involved in the analysis was 27,607.

The results of this analysis revealed some positive associations between general academic performance (as indicated by average scores in English, maths and science GCSE examinations, and the average score in non-arts GCSE subjects) and the taking of arts-based courses, especially for music. However, some negative associations were also apparent (e.g. between GCSE maths scores and the taking of art or drama), and evidence emerged to suggest that pupils who took a higher proportion of arts-related subjects (e.g. more than one of the three arts subjects) were associated with reduced general academic attainment at GCSE. Further analyses showed that the relationships varied significantly between schools.

The report discussed whether the findings should be seen as an indication of the impact of taking arts-related subjects on GCSE attainment or as signalling the effect of predicted GCSE performance on the take-up of arts subjects in the light of pupils' academic attainment and experiences during key stage 3. If confirmed, this latter interpretation raises important issues about the place of the arts in curriculum options systems and the influences on pupils' choices, including their perceptions of the relevance and status of the arts.

CONCLUDING COMMENT

Overall, while the early results from the case-study interviews with teachers and pupils offer testimony to the magnitude and potency of the direct effects of quality provision in the arts, initial and exploratory analyses of the quantitative data suggest that caution is warranted regarding claims about some of the possible indirect or transfer effects. However, because the study is still in its early stages, these findings are very tentative and provisional – all the interpretations offered are subject to further scrutiny in the subsequent phases of the research.

REFERENCES

DEPARTMENT OF NATIONAL HERITAGE (1996). *Setting the Scene: The Arts and Young People.* London: Department of National Heritage.

DU PONT, S. (1992). 'The effectiveness of creative drama as an instructional strategy to enhance the reading skills of fifth graders', *Reading Research and Instruction*, **31**, 3, 41-52.

EISNER, E. (1998). 'Does experience in the arts boost academic achievement?', *Art Education*, **51**, 1, 7-15.

FORSETH, S. (1980). 'Arts activities, attitudes and achievement in elementary mathematics', *Studies in Art Education*, **21**, 2, 22-7.

FOX, A. and GARDINER, M.L. (1997). 'The arts and raising achievement'. Paper presented at The Arts in the Curriculum Conference, organised by the Department of the National Heritage and the School Curriculum and Assessment Authority on 25 February.

GARDINER, M.F., FOX, A., KNOWLES, F. and JEFFRY, D. (1996). 'Learning improved by arts training', *Nature*, **381**, 23 May, 284.

HARLAND, J., KINDER, K. AND HARTLEY, K. (1995). *Arts in Their View: A Study of Youth Participation in the Arts.* Slough: NFER.

KOKAS, K. (1969). 'Psychological testing in Hungarian music education', *Journal of Research in Music Education*, **17**, 1, 125-32.

LUFTIG, R.L. (1994). The Schooled Mind: Do the Arts Make a Difference? An Empirical Evaluation of the Hamilton Fairfield SPECTRA+ Program, 1992-93. Oxford, Ohio: Center for Human Development, Learning and Teaching, Miami University.

RAUSCHER, F.H., SHAW, G.L., LEVINE, L.J., WRIGHT, E.L., DENNIS, W.R. and NEWCOMB, R.L. (1997). 'Music training causes long-term enhancement of preschool children's spatial-temporal reasoning', *Neurological Research*, **19**, February, 2-7.

ROGERS, R. (1995). *Guaranteeing an Entitlement to the Arts in Schools.* London: The Royal Society for the encouragement of Arts, Manufactures and Commerce.

ROSS, M. and KAMBA, M. (1997). *The State of The Arts in Five Secondary Schools.* Exeter: University of Exeter.

SCHAGEN, I. (1996). *Quantitative Analysis for Self-Evaluation.* Slough: NFER.

SCHOOL CURRICULUM AND ASSESSMENT AUTHORITY. (1997). *The Arts in the Curriculum*. A joint conference held by the School Curriculum and Assessment Authority and the Department of National Heritage. London: School Curriculum and Assessment Authority.

SHARP, C. (1998). *The Effects of Teaching and Learning in the Arts: A Review of Research*. London: QCA and NFER.

SPYCHIGER, M., PATRY, J-L., LAUPER, G., ZIMMERMANN, E. and WEBER, E. (1995). 'Does more music teaching lead to a better social climate?' In: OLECHOWSKI, R and KHAN-SVIK, G. (Eds) *Experimental Research on Teaching and Learning*. Frankfurt: Peter Lang.

WOLFF, K. (1978). 'The non-musical outcomes of music education: a review of the literature', *Bulletin of the Council of Research in Music Education*, **55**, 1-27.

APPENDIX I

The Effects and Effectiveness of Arts Education in Secondary Schools: An RSA and NFER Research Project

Introduction

In 1995, the RSA (The Royal Society for the encouragement of Arts, Manufactures and Commerce) published its report *Guaranteeing an Entitlement to the Arts in Schools* (Rogers, 1995). Since then, the Society's reputation for contributing to the debate and influencing the future of the arts in schools has grown. The references to its work in the DNH's *Setting the Scene* (Department of National Heritage, 1996) demonstrate that, not only has the RSA had a significant influence on the recommendations in this policy document, but it is an important advocate for the arts, particularly for the arts in education.

If the RSA exists, in the words of its founder, to '*embolden enterprise, to refine art, to improve our manufactures and to extend commerce*', then part of this mission must be to aid the establishment of a healthy and strong arts education in our schools, which will enable young people, particularly at key stage 4, to experience a broad and relevant arts curriculum. However, in order to substantiate the case for the arts in the curriculum, there is a clear need for valid and impartially collected evidence on the outcomes of arts education in schools. To help achieve this, the RSA, as part of its 'The Arts Matter Initiative', has launched an independent research project, which the NFER will conduct.

Background

Little research has been done in the UK on the effects of arts education and their relation to the processes associated with arts teaching and provision. Although numerous valuable evaluations of individual arts projects and initiatives in schools have been undertaken, they have tended to focus on processes rather than outcomes and have rarely examined the cumulative effects of involvement in arts education. The absence of a comprehensive and empirically based theoretical framework for conceptualising such effects is particularly noticeable.

In order to address this largely neglected yet important area, this research will seek to identify the effects of arts education and will examine the relationship between these effects and a wide range of factors and processes associated with arts provision in schools. The study, which is planned as a three-year investigation, will take account of intended and unintended outcomes, as well as the relationship between these effects and the schools' expressed aims and values. In recognition of the possible extrinsic benefits which an arts education may offer, the project will include an examination of any associations between pupils' participation in the arts and their general academic achievement. This line of inquiry will allow the research to contribute to the growing number of studies in other countries that are exploring the wider gains in learning that may accrue from experiences in arts education (for example in Switzerland and Germany, research is now in progress on the effects of music lessons on developments in language and social skills).

Aims

The study will aim to:

(i)   document and evidence the range of effects and outcomes attributable to school-based arts education;

(ii)   examine the relationship between these effects and the key factors and processes associated with arts provision in schools;

(iii)   illuminate good practice in schools' provision of high-quality educational experiences in the arts; and

(iv)   study the extent to which high levels of institutional involvement in the arts correlate with the qualities known to be associated with successful school improvement and school effectiveness.

Methods

In order to produce research findings which can be statistically robust and yet subtly expositive, the study will use both quantitative and qualitative methods. Three annual phases of research are planned.

Phase 1

- Case studies. Five secondary schools will be invited to become case studies for the focus of the qualitative work. This sample will consist of schools which have a reputation for good practice in the provision of arts education. Two cohorts of pupils (Year 7 and 9) will be interviewed about their arts experiences. Other interviewees will include senior and middle managers, teachers of arts and other subjects, and LEA personnel. Observations of classroom practice will also be conducted.

- Analysis of existing QUASE data. This element will analyse information collected by NFER's 'Quantitative Analysis for Self-Evaluation' project on input and outcome scores for school leaver cohorts. Sub-samples of overachievers and underachievers will be identified and analyses will examine the extent to which pupils in these sub-samples had taken arts-oriented GCSE courses.

- Piloting a Year 11 pupil survey. The case-study schools will be used to pilot a Year 11 pupil questionnaire, which will be administered to a larger sample of schools in Phase Two.

Phase 2
- Case studies. Continuation of the fieldwork in the five case-study schools, including further interviews with the two pupil cohorts.

- The Year 11 pupil survey. Before completing their GCSE examinations, Year 11 pupils in a sample of schools will be requested to provide information on their experiences in, and attitudes to the arts. Analyses will investigate the relation between these variables, biographical information, the taking of GCSE courses in the arts and performance in GCSE examinations.

- Piloting the wider community survey. Interviews among the wider school community, including employers and former pupils.

Phase 3
- Case studies. Completing the fieldwork in the five schools, including the final interviews with the longitudinal pupil cohorts.

- An employer and employee survey. As piloted in Phase 2, a telephone interview survey on the relevance of the arts to the world of work.

Outcomes

An annual report on each phase will present interim findings, with an overall report at the completion of the project. Various dissemination events will be organised during the course of the project, including an international seminar to consider this research and similar projects now taking place in other countries (e.g. USA, Australia, Germany and Switzerland).

Project information

PROJECT DIRECTOR	John Harland
PROJECT LEADER	Kay Kinder
PROJECT TEAM	Mary Ashworth
	Jo Haynes
SECRETARIES	Sue Medd
	Sally Wilson
SPONSORS	Arts Council of England, Association for Business Sponsorship of the Arts, Calouste Gulbenkian Foundation, Comino Foundation, CLEA (Council for Local Education Authorities) Annual Research Programme, Crayola Ltd., and Powys LEA
DURATION	February 1997-March 2000

For further information about the research, please contact:
John Harland or Kay Kinder,
NFER Northern Office,
Genesis 4,
York Science Park,
University Road,
Heslington,
York YO10 5DG
Telephone: (01904) 433435 Fax: (01904) 433436   E-mail: jbh3@york.ac.uk